MANAGING NERVOUSNESS AS A PUBLIC SPEAKER

FIRST EDITION

Edited by Dr. Kristopher K. Merceron and Dr. Charles S. Drinnon
Valencia College and Central Georgia Technical College

Bassim Hamadeh, CEO and Publisher
Jennifer McCarthy, Acquisitions Editor
Michelle Piehl, Project Editor
Berenice Quirino, Associate Production Editor
Miguel Macias, Senior Graphic Designer
Stephanie Kohl, Licensing Associate
Gustavo Youngberg, Interior Designer
Natalie Piccotti, Senior Marketing Manager
Kassie Graves, Vice President of Editorial
Jamie Giganti, Director of Academic Publishing

Copyright © 2019 by Cognella, Inc. All rights reserved. No part of this publication may be reprinted, reproduced, transmitted, or utilized in any form or by any electronic, mechanical, or other means, now known or hereafter invented, including photocopying, microfilming, and recording, or in any information retrieval system without the written permission of Cognella, Inc. For inquiries regarding permissions, translations, foreign rights, audio rights, and any other forms of reproduction, please contact the Cognella Licensing Department at rights@cognella.com.

Trademark Notice: Product or corporate names may be trademarks or registered trademarks, and are used only for identification and explanation without intent to infringe.

Cover image copyright© 2016 iStockphoto LP/HAYKIRDI.

Printed in the United States of America.

ISBN: 978-1-5165-2717-5 (pbk) / 978-1-5165-2718-2 (br)

MANAGING NERVOUSNESS AS A PUBLIC SPEAKER

FIRST EDITION

TABLE OF CONTENTS

INTRODUCTION   VII

CHAPTER 1: WHAT IS NERVOUSNESS & ANXIETY?   1

   Reading 1: Anxiety   3
      by Doris Iarovici

CHAPTER 2: CAN ANXIETY BE GOOD?   21

   Reading 2: Make Friends with Anxiety   22
      by Marvin Weisbord and Sandra Janoff

CHAPTER 3: THE BIOLOGY OF NERVOUSNESS   39

   Reading 3: The Consequences of Stress   40
      by Jolynn Gardner

CHAPTER 4: THE PSYCHOLOGY OF NERVOUSNESS   57

   Reading 4: Fear: Can't Live with It, Can't live without It   59
      by Scott O. Lilienfeld

   Reading 5: Responsiveness to a Mindfulness Manipulation Predicts Affect Regarding an Anger-Provoking Situation   67
      by Catherine N. M. Ortner and Philip David Zelazo

CHAPTER 5: NERVOUSNESS AND PUBLIC SPEAKING   **85**

    Reading 6: Default Public Speaking Settings   87
        by Steven D. Cohen

CHAPTER 6: MEDITATION AND MINDFULNESS   **93**

    Reading 7: Creating the Conditions for Growth and Learning   94
        by Lina Lanestrand

CHAPTER 7: BUILDING CONFIDENCE   **105**

    Reading 8: Deliver Your Message with Confidence and Impact   106
        by Paul R. Timm and Sherron Bienvenu

CHAPTER 8: ARE YOU READY TO SPEAK PUBLICLY?   **143**

    Reading 9: Pause and Refresh—Relax, You'll Do Fine   144
        by Association for Talent Development

INTRODUCTION

Managing Nervousness as a Public Speaker is a text created to provide a deeper understanding of the intricacies of public speaker nervousness. The text walks a reader through answering the first question of "What is nervousness?" and into the various biological and psychological effects nervousness has on a speaker. Furthermore, the text aims to provide the reader with the knowledge and strategies needed to manage nervousness as public speakers. This text is meant to supplement current core public speaking textbooks by providing further exploration into public speaker nervousness and anxiety. This exploration consists of a discussion of the physiological perspective of nervousness and how nervousness can be manipulated and leveraged for a speaker's benefit.

Managing Nervousness as a Public Speaker is a necessary text in today's market because nervousness and anxiety in public speaking is rarely comprehensively covered in most public speaking textbooks or in most public speaking courses. It is the opinion of the text authors that students are not receiving enough insight into understanding what nervousness is, how it looks, and its impacts upon their public speaking. The authors of this text believe that providing students with the information and insight contained in this textbook will give students a much better understanding of what their own individual anxiety looks like and how an individual can leverage and overcome anxiety, which will allow a student to improve public speaking performance. The text also delves into discussions of subjects such as deep breathing and meditation, confidence building, and self-reflection through the lens of a public speaker.

After reading this text, readers will develop a better understanding of what their own individual nervousness looks like and possess the tools needed to leverage and channel their anxiety into positive energy they can use in becoming a more effective public speaker. The material in this text provides the reader with in-depth explanations of various concepts associated with nervousness and anxiety, exercises for readers to employ on their own to help with practice and repetition, and additional references and readings to add context and reinforcement to the material presented in the text. Although *Managing Nervousness as a Public Speaker* supplements public speaking textbooks, this text can be utilized by students, teachers, professionals, and everyday individuals seeking to strengthen their own public speaking skills and understand their own nervousness or to even educate others to help them achieve similar goals.

CHAPTER 1

WHAT IS NERVOUSNESS & ANXIETY?

Chapter 1 begins by asking the essential question: "What is nervousness and anxiety?" This is one of the first questions that should be asked when beginning the journey to better understanding your own anxiety and leveraging it to strengthen your public speaking skills. In reading one, from Doris Iarovici's book *Mental Health Issues and the University Student* (2014), she states, "Anxiety and fear are universal human emotions, with significant adaptive functions in our lives" (p. 126). This means that these emotions play a vital role in our lives, especially in regard to speaking publicly; however, what exactly is anxiety and nervousness?

Anxiety can be defined as a multifaceted human response to particular situations; this response can take on both biological and psychological forms. Biologically, a person experiencing anxiety may exhibit sweaty palms, arms, and face; nausea; dizziness; rapid heart rate; and uncontrolled breathing. Psychologically, a person experiencing anxiety may be in a state of constant worry, self-doubt, or insecurity and may have an extremely negative perspective on the experience or task causing the anxiety. These manifestations of anxiety will be discussed further in later chapters and is also covered in the reading: "Fear: Can't Live with It, Can't Live without It."

So, if a person can experience all of this, how does nervousness factor into a person's life? Before answering this question, let's take a look at the different types of anxiety. Anxiety can take many different forms, from developmentally normal or short-lived situational anxiety to a debilitating anxiety disorder, which requires professional, and sometimes medical, intervention. Understanding the differences between the various forms of anxiety can help you better comprehend your own nervousness and how it impacts your life. Developmentally normal or short-lived situational anxiety can sometimes occur in individuals experiencing an unfamiliar event, task, or group. In these situations, which are typically short-term or temporary, individuals may feel anxious and exhibit some of the different biological and psychological factors spoken about previously. This form of anxiety is very common as we experience unfamiliar or even uncomfortable situations, but since these situations are temporary, they do not maintain lasting negative effects on our mind or body. As the experience comes to an end, you begin to feel a sense of relaxation as your mind and body begin to calm themselves down.

Short-lived situational anxiety is typically not debilitating nor indicative of long-term negative impacts on the person's mind or body. This form of anxiety is a normal developmental experience most people go through. For example, when reengaging oneself in the same situation multiple times (i.e., delivering a speech in a public speaking class), with each time, you become more and more comfortable. Many times, speakers begin to see a significant decrease in this sense of anxiety as they are faced with this task. As time passes, what was once anxiety might even change to enjoyment and excitement because as our ability to overcome anxiety increases, our satisfaction about overcoming anxiety also increases.

ANXIETY

by Doris Iarovici

Anxiety and fear are universal human emotions, with significant adaptive functions in our lives. But surveys of college students suggest that in the past decade or two, more are experiencing problematic anxiety. Nearly half of students in the 2011 National College Health Assessment Survey reported experiencing "overwhelming anxiety" within the past year.[1] Some of these were likely facing developmentally normal or short-lived situational anxiety, but others may have been suffering from an anxiety disorder. Clearly anxiety, or stress, as a presenting concern in counseling centers is on the rise, endorsed by 63% of counseling center patients in 2001, compared with only 36% in 1988.[2] It has become the most commonly cited concern among counseling center clients. Untreated, anxiety can become a chronic, debilitating problem. But most anxiety disorders as well as more self-limited developmental anxieties respond well to treatment, especially in emerging adults, who rapidly grasp the concepts of what causes anxiety and how to most effectively approach rather than avoid the problems it can cause.

Doris Iarovici, "Anxiety," *Mental Health Issues and the University Student*, pp. 126-139, 233-234. Copyright © 2014 by Johns Hopkins University Press. Reprinted with permission.

DIAGNOSIS: REGULAR WORRY VERSUS A DISORDER

Mike is a 24-year-old African American second-year medical student from Seattle who comes in complaining of declining academic performance and concerns about whether he has chosen the right profession. He describes feeling a constant sense of dread about school, racing thoughts, difficulty falling asleep, and frequent stomach disturbances. It's hard to face the day. He can't stop obsessing about whether he should be in medical school or not and often thinks about this question while on hospital rounds, causing him to miss questions that the attending physician directs to him. His mind often goes blank during presentations, and his hands tremble if he's holding notes, making him feel unprepared and embarrassed. He's been told to "relax" by several supervisors and has tried to, but to no avail. He was an excellent student as an undergraduate but has not been able to make honors in any of his medical school courses thus far, and he feels ashamed and demoralized by this. He's most afraid that he will fail to take proper care of his patients and flunk out.

Academic demands occasionally trigger anxiety for most students, but when anxiety is sustained and debilitating, an anxiety disorder may be to blame. Among American adults, anxiety disorders are the most common psychiatric illnesses, with a prevalence rate of 13% to 18%.[3] There's less data on the rate of all anxiety disorders among college students. One study found that in a sample of nearly 3,000 undergraduate and graduate students at a large midwestern university, 4.2% screened positive for either generalized anxiety disorder (GAD) or panic disorder based on the PHQ-9 questionnaire, with GAD being the more common diagnosis.[4] In this study, more women than men suffered from anxiety (mirroring the general population), and more than a third who had anxiety also had some form of depression. One-fifth of those who screened positive for GAD also had suicidal thoughts.

Students frequently use the word "stress" to describe anxiety, though at times it may also refer to depressive symptoms. It's important to get a clear picture of exactly what they mean. Do they feel nervous, tense, afraid, anxious? Is there a sense of physical restlessness or irritability? How long and in what contexts have they been noticing this? Mike also uses the word "obsessing," as students frequently do, but it's helpful to distinguish between occasional irrational worries or constant excessive worries about usual life events, which more typically suggest generalized anxiety, and true obsessive thoughts, which are intrusive, often ego-dystonic, sometimes bizarre or embarrassing, and more commonly accompanied by compulsions. In DSM-5, obsessive-compulsive disorder is separated from the anxiety disorders chapter. Had Mike described a constant thought that he might harm his patients, for example, or intrusive images of actually harming patients, an OCD-spectrum diagnosis may have been more likely.

Other psychiatric conditions can cause or mimic anxiety. The complaint of "racing thoughts" is common among students, and it's important to clarify whether this is an anxiety symptom or a manic or hypomanic one. A newly emerging psychosis can also cause significant anxiety. Anxiety disorders have high rates of comorbidity with other psychiatric problems—especially, for college students, substance abuse.

Mike describes uncertainty over career choice, a developmentally common concern for both graduate and undergraduate students. Probing the specifics of this is important. Did he go to medical school to please family? Did other external or cultural reasons turn him toward a career for which he has little passion? Or is an underlying anxiety problem making him second-guess every decision in his life, thus interfering with his ability to enjoy what perhaps *is* his own chosen path? Would insight-oriented psychotherapy focusing on his hopes and dreams help him untangle this, or is it more appropriate to proceed with cognitive behavioral therapy, more narrowly targeting the anxiety symptoms? And what about medications?

Many of these questions are best addressed through a flexible, creative, and collaborative approach that presents the student with choices for treatment and acknowledges the complexity of his presentation at this time. Diagnostic clarity will also help guide the treatment recommendations. (See figure 1.1 for an algorithm on evaluating anxiety.) Students sometimes present with symptoms across several of the anxiety disorders, without meeting full diagnostic criteria for any one in particular; asking screening questions for all the anxiety disorders should help refine the diagnostic impression. Screening inventories such as the Beck Anxiety Inventory or the Yale-Brown Obsessive-Compulsive Scale can be useful not only in clarifying diagnosis, but also in monitoring treatment response.

> Mike admits he has been a worrier much of his life, though it caused him few problems before in school or in relationships. He denies having been particularly shy and in fact describes himself as "easygoing" prior to medical school. He found life on the West Coast more laid back and dealt with feelings of restlessness or tension when they occurred by hiking or participating in sports, or by socializing with his friends in Seattle. None of these outlets are as readily available at his east Coast medical school. He did frequently daydream as a child and adolescent

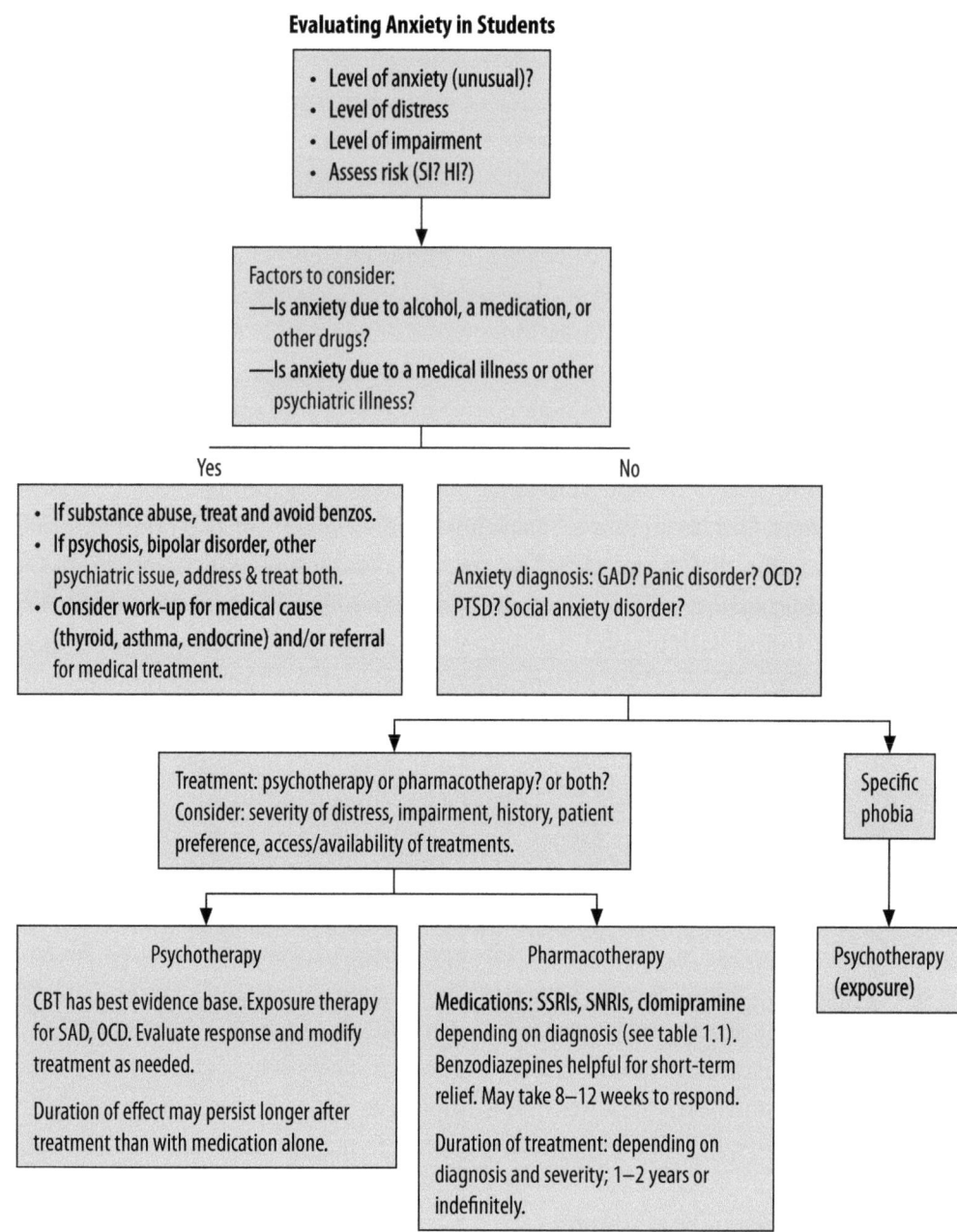

Figure 1.1. Evaluating Anxiety in Students.

Source: Adapted from American Psychiatric Association Practice Guidelines and Swinson R. P., Antony, M. M., Bleau, P. B., et al. (2006), "Clinical Practice Guidelines: Management of Anxiety *Disorders.*" *Canadian Journal of Psychiatry, 51* (suppl 2): 1–92.

but was not hyperactive. Although good at science, he double-majored in philosophy and biology and enjoyed thinking deeply. He finds the amount of material in medical school daunting and the content somewhat boring, and he feels "slow" compared to peers. He was worried and tense through much of his first year of medical school, but all these symptoms abated at home over the summer in Seattle. He denies a trauma history or panic attacks, but in addition to hands shaking and mind going blank during presentations, he has tachycardia and flushing. He denies wanting to harm himself but has been more preoccupied with thoughts of death and feeling like he's not sure there's a point to life.

GENERALIZED ANXIETY DISORDER AND SOCIAL ANXIETY DISORDER

In differentiating developmental anxiety from an anxiety disorder, consider severity and duration of symptoms, context, and impairment. Mike's difficult-to-control worry has been interfering with his academic performance for about 18 months and is intensifying rather than abating. If it were simply a matter of considering his career choice, he might have been able to work through it by now and make a decision, but he worries about several career-related questions and is unable to move forward with any changes. Excessive worry alone is not sufficient to diagnose generalized anxiety disorder (GAD), and in fact studies show that a significant proportion of college students worry excessively but most don't have GAD. One large study that compared undergraduates who were "high worriers" with and without GAD found that the GAD high worriers worried more days than not—more frequently than the non-GAD high worriers—and felt less control over their worry, felt greater impairment specifically due to the worry, and suffered muscle tension and feelings of restlessness significantly more frequently than non-GAD high worriers.[5]

The clinical picture for Mike is most suggestive of generalized anxiety disorder: pervasive worry, muscle tension, sleep difficulties, and mind going blank. DSM-5 reports that GAD is more frequently encountered in adults of European rather than non-European descent, and in women more than men. The literature describes GAD as a chronic condition that persists across contexts, but in my experience working with students, it's not unusual for symptoms to occur at school and then diminish during summers or semesters away from campus. It's almost as if for some people, there's a level of anxiety that simmers just below the diagnostic threshold, and the substantial demands of college or graduate school tip the balance toward the full boil of a clinical problem.

In addition to academic demands, college and graduate or professional school place physical and social demands on emerging adults. Medical school in particular is notorious for interfering with sleep and eating routines. The culture of medicine is one of intense focus on work, with students' mentors frequently modeling poor self-care. We often have to remind students in the healing professions to also take care of their own health, in order to be well enough to care for others.

Anxiety can interfere with working memory, and even students without generalized anxiety often complain of test anxiety or performance anxiety. Again, the need for clinical intervention rests on the severity of impairment. Mike describes several physiological symptoms of performance anxiety that do impair his learning, and that should respond well to treatment. Most likely, anxiety is compromising his academic functioning, but it's also worthwhile to consider whether he might have undiagnosed ADHD. Though it would be unusual for someone to perform so well academically that they're admitted to medical school and still have an undiagnosed learning issue, it's not impossible.

Mike's significant performance anxiety might be considered a variant of social phobia, or social anxiety disorder, nongeneralized subtype, although its absence from earlier periods of his life is intriguing. Is he part of a racial minority group at his medical school, and if so, in what way might this experience affect his confidence and social ease? Some minority students describe the pressure of being the "token" whose performance must stand in for the capabilities of a whole group of people. Even for some nonminority students with an anxious temperament, a poor performance, as the stakes are raised in college or professional school, is so humiliating that they then develop performance anxiety, which abates after treatment, without the need for the more typical ongoing treatment. Had Mike endorsed anxiety in other social situations, he might have been suffering from generalized social anxiety, which afflicts two-thirds of those with social anxiety.[6] Social anxiety disorder is the third most common psychiatric diagnosis in the general population and likely about equally prevalent in campus samples. Interestingly, a study comparing a clinical sample of college students to a nonclinical sample (students taking a psychology class) found similar rates of social phobia based on responses to the Social Phobia Inventory, suggesting that social phobia might be developmentally more common—and thus perhaps not always a disorder—in this population.[7] After all, authors and artists across time have described the social awkwardness and group anxieties of adolescents as they grow into their own areas of comfort with self and peers; these appear quite common in the college years too.

Students with generalized anxiety often have many physical complaints, especially gastrointestinal ones. one large study of undergraduates at UCLA found that of the students who were diagnosed with irritable bowel syndrome (IBS), over 21% also met criteria for GAD, compared with only 7% of students without IBS.[8] Headaches and muscle tension are also frequent complaints. With treatment, many of these symptoms improve along with the psychological symptoms.

ANXIETY AND IDENTITY

> Louise, an 18-year-old Caucasian sophomore from Alabama, comes in complaining of crying spells, fatigue, and loss of interest in cheerleading. She's a member of the college's prestigious cheerleading squad, which guarantees an active social life, but she usually feels like she's just going through the motions and skips social events whenever she can. She was a shy teenager with a very outgoing mother who made sure she was actively involved in the "right kinds" of social activities during high school. She avoids speaking in class, avoids classes that require participation as part of the grade, and suffers significant physiological arousal when she does have to speak up. Cheering isn't hard for her because, she explains, "it's not really me when I'm out there—it's all an act." When asked about friendships and romances, she flushes and says, "and that's another problem. I think I might be bisexual and have a crush on a girl. But I totally don't fit into the whole LGBT scene here, and my family would make me transfer if they knew."

Social anxiety disorder doesn't discriminate—it can affect students who don't, on the surface, appear to be shy or socially isolated. Sometimes it affects the popular fraternity vice president who quells his panic attacks in new social situations with a case of beer, or the pretty cheerleader whom other students see as conformist and popular. Louise illustrates other complexities that arise in diagnosing anxiety in students: she is in the midst of exploring her own sexual orientation and feels unsupported in this in both her family and her campus community. College is a time when students can shed parts of their identity that may not fit them, and this often brings on or exacerbates anxiety. College is also a time when students grapple with existential questions about the meaning of life and their role in the world. Students need clinicians who are open to exploring these questions with them without pathologizing or rushing past them.

For Louise, hiding certain aspects of her identity can account for her anxiety around people she doesn't know well, and the anxiety might abate as she feels more comfortable and can more authentically express herself. However, there's also evidence that the rate of anxiety (and mood) disorders differs according to sexual orientation, with different patterns for men and women. For women who identify as bisexual, the lifetime rates of mood or anxiety disorders are twice as high as for heterosexual women; there are similarly higher rates for bisexual and gay men, but women who are attracted to and have had sex exclusively with women actually have the lowest rates of these psychiatric issues, controlling for other demographic variables.[9]

Emerging adults are also working on other issues of identity formation that can cause anxiety, especially if in conflict with family of origin values and norms. Students may have various other experiences of oppression on campus. Students in racial, ethnic, or religious minority groups may feel isolated or socially awkward due to interacting with people or in situations that differ greatly from what they have previously encountered. International students who were not in a minority group in their home country may suddenly feel intense anxiety accompanying their new experience of being in a minority group on the American campus. It's important to consider these variables in distinguishing "normal" anxiety from the "disorders." At the same time, even students experiencing oppression may have a co-occurring anxiety disorder. A careful patient history, asking if symptoms were ever experienced in the home country or in other home environments; family history; and focus on current impairment can help tease these apart.

OBSESSIVE-COMPULSIVE SPECTRUM SYMPTOMS

Sometimes, a student who complains of being newly "slower" at completing work than classmates, as Mike did in the vignette above, might be rigidly perfectionistic or procrastinating out of fear of doing poorly. But in some instances this complaint may uncover an obsessive preoccupation with getting things done "just so" or with another intrusive thought that distracts the student. It occasionally can be due to compulsive behaviors or mental rituals, such as the need to count letters in words to have them "even up." Students may misattribute their behavior to being particularly conscientious or thorough, but in some cases their rereading or need to write a perfect sentence prevents them from completing assignments at all, or else causes them to spend untenable amounts of time on simple tasks. Using a scale, such as the Yale-Brown Obsessive-Compulsive Scale (Y-BOCS) can help clarify diagnosis and also monitor treatment efficacy.

According to the National Institute of Mental Health, obsessive-compulsive disorder (OCD) has a lifetime prevalence of about 2% in emerging adults.[10] But among emerging adults in college, higher rates have been reported, especially if we're looking not only at full-criteria OCD but also at the spectrum of symptoms that are fairly common on campus. There's increasing recognition of and interest in obsessive-compulsive-like symptoms and disorders, including body dysmorphic disorder (when an individual is excessively preoccupied with a body part), trichotillomania (hair pulling), pathological skin picking, and health anxiety or hypochondriasis. This group of disorders is now listed in its own category in DSM-5, separately from the anxiety disorders. This is meant to encourage clinicians to also consider the other disorders when one in the cluster seems to be affecting someone. Because OCD has a strong genetic component and because people with OCD have significantly higher rates of other anxiety disorders, some researchers recommended leaving OCD within the anxiety disorders category.[11] Instead, the DSM-5 acknowledges the close relationship between OCD and the other anxiety disorders by listing OCD in the section immediately following the anxiety disorders section.

In my experience, obsessions and compulsions are fairly frequent among college students, and although they don't always rise to the level of a disorder, they cause impairment and thus remain important to assess and address in the course of treatment. A recent study of college students supported this. In a nonclinical volunteer undergraduate sample, some symptoms of an OCD-related disorder were quite common. The authors report that "22% experienced hair pulling urges, and 30% spent at least an hour a day obsessing over a perceived physical flaw or engaged in activities related to this flaw (e.g., staring in the mirror, covering up the flaw)."[12] Perhaps more surprising was that in this sample of students, the rates of symptoms that suggested a full-blown disorder were fairly high. Based on self-report questionnaires, 5% of students met OCD criteria, 5% qualified for a body dysmorphic disorder diagnosis, 3% for trichotillomania, 6% for pathological skin picking, 7% for health anxiety, and these rates were reportedly consistent with rates seen in other studies of college students. Most of the students who qualified for a diagnosis also showed increased overall anxiety compared with students without an OCD-related disorder, and those with pathological skin picking and trichotillomania also had increased impulsivity scores. Thus these are relatively common symptoms in students, and many who experience them are adversely affected but may never seek help.

PANIC, POST-TRAUMATIC STRESS, AND PHOBIAS

Occasional unexpected panic attacks are fairly common among college students. In one large nonclinical undergraduate sample, 12% had experienced a panic attack in their lifetime; 2.6% had diagnosable panic disorder.[13] That same study found that although women report more panic attacks, men actually worry more about panic and thus in college samples may be equally at risk for developing panic disorder. Students who experience panic attacks frequently seek help from their physician or the emergency department before they present to a mental health provider, although these days more students are educated about panic and may first come to a counseling center. Panic symptoms are nonspecific and can signal any anxiety disorder, a mood disorder, a substance use disorder, or, more rarely in the college-aged population, a physical health problem. Sometimes they're situational and self-limited, and educating the student about the nature of the symptoms can prevent the anticipatory anxiety about having more panic, preventing the progression to panic disorder.

Panic also often accompanies various phobias, such as fear of flying. Students who present with the latter sometimes have quite constrained college experiences because of their fears: they may drive cross-country to school rather than fly, and avoid semester-or summer-abroad experiences or limit their postgraduate plans based on avoiding flight. Students who develop agoraphobia while on campus can suffer significant academic consequences, skipping class and being perceived as unmotivated.

The college years are considered a high-risk time for exposure to traumatic experiences as well. In surveys, most college students report having experienced at least one traumatic event when the definition of trauma includes death or life-threatening illness of a loved one or accidents. Most of these students, however, don't develop the difficult and sometimes debilitating symptoms of post-traumatic stress disorder (PTSD). Interestingly, there's a discrepancy between the types of trauma that students consider "worst" and the traumas that seem to cause the most symptoms. Sexual assault caused the greatest incidence of PTSD in one large study of college students, yet of the students who'd experienced it, only slightly more than a third rated it as their "worst ever" trauma.[14] Women and racial minority students reported more lifetime traumatic events than male and white students, highlighting the need to remain sensitive to differential risk among different students.

Since the number of international students on campus has dramatically increased, and since some of these students hail from regions of the world with significant violence or war, we may also see increases in PTSD among this student subgroup, though systematic research is lacking. And as more American-born students travel to regions of the world that are in conflict, or return to campus after serving in the Gulf wars, we may see increases in students suffering combat-related PTSD. Academic programs that immerse undergraduate students in different cultures sometimes inadvertently also expose them to experiences of vicarious traumatization, without adequate emotional preparation in advance or opportunities for debriefing once they return to campus. For example, one young student who returned from an academic experience where she interviewed women who'd survived an ethnic cleansing experience had significant psychological symptoms long after her return to campus, even though she didn't experience or directly witness the traumatic events.

TREATMENT CONSIDERATIONS

The good news for both Mike and Louise in the vignettes above is that there are several evidence-based treatment approaches for anxiety disorders, and early intervention often changes the entire course of a student's progression through school. For all students, the opportunity to discuss their fears and learn healthier ways of responding to them is invaluable. Of course, specific treatment will depend on the specific nature and severity of the problem. Because there is so much diagnostic overlap between the anxiety disorders, I worry less about a specific diagnostic code and instead try to understand the nature and patterns of the anxiety.

If a student's anxiety seems short lived and mostly situational, then simple relaxation techniques, breathing exercises, and reassurance may be all that's needed. Education about the nature of anxiety and how avoidance reinforces it, while action and exposure can extinguish it also goes a long way with intelligent, self-motivated students. Some of these interventions can be delivered in a group format. At Duke we regularly offer brief (one- to three-session) workshops on "worrying well" and stress management. We also offer regular mindfulness meditation groups, and although these are not specifically targeted to anxiety, they often significantly reduce worry. Advertising these to the entire campus community, rather than reserving these groups only for clinicians' referrals, allows a broader range of students to participate and to benefit.

Even in students dealing with situational or short-lived anxiety, if sleep impairment is present, then we address it directly. Sometimes a focus on sleep hygiene will be sufficient (with written instructions to the student), but sometimes, a short course of either a hypnotic agent or a low-dose benzodiazepine is invaluable in breaking a cycle of worry and insomnia. Because college students with anxiety frequently turn to alcohol or drugs as coping mechanisms, any comorbid substance use must be addressed through a combination of education and motivational interviewing.

A student like Mike or Louise likely needs a more intensive treatment approach. CBT is effective for all the anxiety disorders. Specific manualized treatments for each disorder can be helpful, as can group treatment approaches. Although the evidence is strongest for CBT groups, for college students, attending to group dynamics may be equally effective. One small study comparing a CBT group for social anxiety to a control group psychotherapy approach based on Yalom and Leszcz found that the control group did just as well on all measures of improvement in social anxiety and actually had less attrition.[15] The control group used more nonspecific group interventions, such as encouraging participants to support each other, and provide feedback on how they perceived each other, and take responsibility for group participation and homework assignments. My own clinical experience resonates with this finding: many socially anxious students have benefitted from general group therapy experiences over the years, including interpersonal groups, grad groups, dissertation support groups, and others, especially when CBT groups specifically targeting anxiety or social anxiety were not available. Since social interactions with peers are such an important developmental task for emerging adults, it makes sense that the exposure to the nonspecific components of group processes, and the ability to receive feedback in the moment, are invaluable to students—once they are finally persuaded to go!

For students with PTSD, those treatments that include some element of an exposure-based CBT are likely to be most helpful, based on recommendations of a 2007 Institute of Medicine review of evidence-based therapies. These exposure-based CBTs include cognitive reprocessing therapy and eye-movement desensitization and reprocessing (EMDR).[16]

Many psychotropic medications are helpful in treating anxiety (table 1.1). Some therapists suggest that psychotherapy should be the first-line treatment, since it's been proven to be effective and safe and since its benefits may last longer after the completion of treatment than those of medications. I believe that the decision regarding therapy or medicine (or both) should be guided by the student's level of distress and impairment, personal and family mental health history, and student preference. A concern is that if a medication is helpful, the student may then have to take that medication indefinitely to maintain wellness. Students themselves, especially anxious students, also worry a lot about dependence on medicine and possible side effects. Anxious students tend to be more worried about taking any medicine and are so attuned to every side effect that it can be hard to simply have a medication trial of adequate dose and duration. Their concerns are all valid and should be addressed respectfully and comprehensively.

Table 1.1 Pharmacological treatment of anxiety disorders

ANXIETY DISORDER	FIRST-LINE TREATMENT	ALTERNATIVES	ADJUVANT
Generalized anxiety disorder	SSRIs, venlafaxine ER	buspirone	clonazepam, lorazepam
Social anxiety disorder	SSRIs (esp. sertraline, escitalopram, fluvoxamine)	venlafaxine ER, fluoxetine	clonazepam, alprazolam, beta-blockers for performance anxiety
PTSD	SSRIs, SNRIs	phenelzine	risperidone, prazosin
OCD	SSRIs, clomipramine	venlafaxine ER	atypical antipsychotics?*
Panic disorder	SSRIs, SNRIs (venlafaxine ER, duloxetine)	tricyclics	alprazolam, clonazepam, lorazepam (consider standing dose at first)

Source: adapted from Guideline Watch. (2013, March). *APA practice guidelines for the treatment of patients with obsessive-compulsive disorder;* Guideline Watch. (2009, March). *Practice guideline for the treatment of patients with acute stress disorder and posttraumatic stress disorder* and *Practice guideline for the treatment of patients with panic disorder* (2nd ed.); and Swinson, R. P., Antony, M. M., & Bleau, P. B., et al. (2006). "Clinical Practice Guidelines: Management of anxiety Disorders." *Canadian Journal of Psychiatry, 51* (suppl. 2): 1–92.
*The evidence is mixed for atypical antipsychotic treatment of OCD.

When a student prefers to start with psychotherapy and has access to it, that is a wonderful first option. Some students have so much anxiety, however, that they can't meaningfully participate in the therapy process. At other times a student lacks sufficient time before an important anxiety-triggering event, such as final exams, to allow therapy to adequately take effect. In these cases I try to ease the student's fears by providing a lot of information about how and why medicines can help, along with my strong professional recommendation (rather than simply providing information on all options and asking the student to make the decision). I always remind them that the choice to take the medicine is entirely theirs, and that they can also choose to stop it at any point.

When treating an anxious student with any medicine, I start low and go slow: low initial dose and slow upward titration to minimize possible side effects. The SSRIs have all shown efficacy in treating GAD, social anxiety disorder, panic disorder, OCD, and PTSD. In general, higher doses usually work better for OCD-spectrum disorders and for PTSD than the doses that seem effective for depression, and it often takes longer to reach the therapeutic effect (for social anxiety disorder and OCD, as long as 8 to 12 weeks). When students have depression comorbid with obsessional symptoms, the depression sometimes improves before the anxiety. Conversely, some very anxious depressed students feel more relaxed starting medicine before they notice mood improvement. Some believe that less severe symptoms improve first.

Short-term use of low-dose, high-potency benzodiazepines can also help students without a history of alcohol or substance abuse, though in PTSD, benzodiazepines can sometimes worsen symptoms. I explain to students the conditioning power of anxiety, and how the fear of loss of control over fear can become a self-fulfilling prophecy. For many students, it's then sufficient to carry around their benzodiazepine and know they can take it if overwhelmed; we discuss this, and often they then find that they don't need to take it.

Although beta blockers were not found to be particularly effective in generalized social anxiety disorder, they can be extremely helpful in cases of disabling performance anxiety. Their use allows students to participate more easily in exposure to feared situations, which ultimately reduces the fear.

Students with a history of significant trauma usually do best in a setting that doesn't impose the kinds of length-of-treatment limits that most college counseling centers must impose. However, sometimes barriers to other care leave the counseling center as the student's only treatment option. In those instances, brief treatment may serve as a bridge to more comprehensive treatment, or medication can provide symptom stabilization.

NOTES

1. American College Health Association. (2011). *American College Health Association–National College Health Assessment Survey: Reference group executive summary, fall 2011.* Linthicum, MD: American College Health Association.

2. Benton, S. A., Robertson, J. M., Tseng, W. C., Newton, F. B., & Benton, S. L. (2003). "Changes in Counseling Center Client Problems across 13 Years." *Professional Psychology: Research and Practice, 34,* 66-72.

3. Cooper, Stewart E. (Ed.). (2005). "Evidence-Based Practice for Anxiety Disorders in College Mental Health." In *Evidence-based psychotherapy practice in college mental health* (pp. 33-48). Philadelphia, PA: Haworth Press. Anxiety and Depression Association of America, www.adaa.org.

4. Eisenberg, D., et al. (2007). "Prevalence and Correlates of Depression, Anxiety and Suicidality among University Students." *American Journal of Orthopsychiatry, 77* (4): 534-42.

5. Ruscio, A. M. (2002). "Delimiting the Boundaries of Generalized Anxiety Disorder: Differentiating High Worriers with and without GAD." *Journal of Anxiety Disorders, 16,* 377-400.

6. Raj, B. A., & Sheehan, D. V. (2001). "Social Anxiety Disorder." *Medical Clinics of North America, 85* (3): 711-33.

7. Stewart, D., & Mandrusiak, M. (2007). "Social Phobia in College Students: A Developmental Perspective." *Journal of College Student Psychotherapy, 22* (2): 49–65.

8. Hazlett-Stevens, H., Craske, M. G., Mayer, E. A., Chang, L., & Naliboff, B. D. (2003). "Prevalence of Irritable Bowel Syndrome among University Students: The Roles of Worry, Neuroticism, Anxiety Sensitivity and Visceral Anxiety." *Journal of Psychosomatic Research, 55,* 501–15.

9. Bostwick, W. B., Boyd, C. J., Hughes, T. L., & McCabe, S. E. (2010). "Dimensions of Sexual Orientation and the Prevalence of Mood and Anxiety Disorders in the United States." *American Journal of Public Health, 100* (3): 468–75.

10. National Institute for Mental Health. "Obsessive Compulsive Disorder among Adults." www.nimh.nih.gov/statistics/1OCD_ADULT.shtml, accessed July 9, 2012.

11. Cowley, Deborah. (2011, June 13). "Is OCD an Anxiety Disorder?" *Journal Watch Psychiatry.*

12. Sulkowski, M. L., Mariaskin, A., & Storch, E. A. (2011). "Obsessive-Compulsive Spectrum Disorder Symptoms in College Students." *Journal of American College Health, 59* (5): 342–48.

13. Tech, M. J., Lucas, J. A., & Nelson, P. (1989). "Nonclinical Panic in College Students: An Investigation of Prevalence and Symptomatology." *Journal of Abnormal Psychology, 98* (3): 300–306.

14. Frazer, P., Anders, S., Sulani, P., Tomich, P., Tennen, H., Park, C., & Tashiro, T. (2009). "Traumatic Events among Undergraduate Students: Prevalence and Associated Symptoms." *Journal of Counseling Psychology, 56* (3): 450–60.

15. Bjornsson, A. S., Bidwell, L. C., Brosse, A. L., Carey, G., Hauser, M., Seghete, K. L. M., Schulz-Heik, R. J., Weatherley, D., Erwin, B. A., & Craighead, W. E. (2011). "Cognitive-Behavioral Group Therapy versus Group Psychotherapy for Social Anxiety Disorder among College Students: A Randomized Controlled Trial." *Depression and Anxiety, 28,* 1034–42. Yalom ID, Leszcz M. (2005). *The theory and practice of group psychotherapy,* 5th ed. New York: Basic Books.

16. Benedek, David M., Friedman, Matthew J., Zatzick, Douglas, & Ursano, Robert J. (2009, March). *Guideline watch: Practice guideline for the treatment of patients with acute stress disorder and posttraumatic stress disorder.* doi:10.1176/appi.books.9780890423479.156498.

CHAPTER SUMMARY

Many aspects of our lives tend to include certain demands that may trigger anxiety, such as education, occupations, families, etc. But when the anxiety becomes debilitating and/or is unrelenting, a person could be experiencing an anxiety disorder. Before discussing anxiety disorders, it is important to understand that many times, we may label situations as stressful or anxiety inducing, but, just as we discussed earlier in this chapter, some of these may be normal, developmental, and temporary. So, when differentiating between "normal" anxiety and an anxiety disorder, Iarovici asks, "Do they feel nervous, tense, afraid, or anxious? Is there a sense of physical restlessness or irritability? How long and in what contexts have they been noticing this?" (p. 127). Questions like these can help you better understand if what you are experiencing is truly a disorder or a developmental episode.

Iarovici tells us, "Among American adults, anxiety disorders are the most common psychiatric illnesses, with a prevalence rate of 13% to 18%" (p. 127), and goes even further to discuss a study that was done with nearly three thousand undergraduate and graduate students. The study found that 4.2% of them had screened positive for either generalized anxiety disorder (GAD) or a panic disorder. With this said, there is a distinct difference between short-term anxiety and an anxiety disorder. For example, when considering a professional path, it is normal to question the reason for choosing law school: for example, whether it was inspired by the desire to please your family or cultural reasons that drive your aspiration to seek that career path. This is normal, especially for a student, to experience when deciding which occupational path they plan to take. When the question becomes "Is [there] an underlying anxiety problem making [you] second-guess every decision in [your] life, thus interfering with [your] ability to enjoy what perhaps *is* [your] own chosen path?" (p. 128), then we begin to consider the possibility of an anxiety disorder.

When considering the presence of an anxiety disorder, one would need to contemplate the severity and duration of the symptoms in addition to the context and the impairment associated with it. Iarovici provides: "Excessive worry alone is not sufficient to diagnose generalized anxiety disorder (GAD), and in fact, studies show that a significant proportion of college students worry excessively but most do not have GAD" (p. 130). When individuals begin to experience muscle tension, sleep complications and deprivation, inescapable and persistent worry, and even excessive loss of train of thought, an anxiety disorder may be the culprit.

When you experience what may be considered an anxiety disorder, it is recommended that you seek out the guidance and consultation of a licensed professional to aid in the diagnosis of your level of the disorder and help to determine potential treatments and/or remedies you can begin to employ in your life. As we have seen a connection between anxiety and stress (and how sometimes it may appear much worse than it actually is), there is also a connection between anxiety and fear. As many know, public speaking is the number one fear in the United States, outranking fear of death and even fear of spiders. This is widely associated with the negative implications anxiety has on public speaking. With this negative connotation associated with public speaking, a significant degree of fear has now become directly related to the act. So, if we know what happens when someone is scared, stressed, or anxious, and there are many different biological and psychological factors associated with it, how can we handle it? Can anxiety be good? This is a question we will answer in chapter 2.

CHAPTER 2

CAN ANXIETY BE GOOD?

In the reading from chapter 2, "Make Friends with Anxiety," you will learn about how to deal with anxiety in its many forms. You will learn that anxiety is normal and can be good. Anxiety can be a source of energy, a source of focus, and a source of strength. You will learn that after overcoming anxiety you will be stronger, tougher, and more able to face future life challenges.

MAKE FRIENDS WITH ANXIETY

by Marvin Weisbord and Sandra Janoff

Nothing in the affairs of men is worthy of great anxiety.

—Plato

Anxiety. Everybody has it. Nobody loves it. Mel Brooks made a movie about it, *High Anxiety* (1977). W. H. Auden wrote a long poem, "The Age of Anxiety" (1947), set in a New York bar. Leonard Bernstein adopted Auden's title for his Symphony No. 2 (1948). We are wallowing in anxiety, generalized, unfocused, nonspecific, and—our favorite term—*free-floating*, a kind of nervous cloud on which we depart the present in a sour mood for a place we'd rather not be. When we put the word *anxiety* into Google, we got 112 million hits in 0.07 second. That's a lot of free-floating anxiety in cyberspace.

ANXIETY—GETTING READY TO LEARN

This chapter has twin themes to help you manage anxiety when you lead meetings that matter. Our first theme is that task-related anxiety can be your best friend. The poet T. S. Eliot called anxiety "the handmaiden of

Marvin Weisbord and Sandra Janoff, "Principle 7: Make Friends with Anxiety," *Don't Just Do Something, Stand There!: Ten Principles for Leading Meetings That Matter*, pp. 119-134, 179-181. Copyright © 2007 by Berrett-Koehler Publishers. Reprinted with permission.

creativity" (or so it says on the Internet). You, too, may discover that apprehension in a meeting often serves as a precursor to creative breakthroughs.

Our second theme is that anxiety provides a wonderful window into your own development. We have learned a great deal about managing our fears and fantasies while leading high-stakes meetings. You can grow your capability for leadership manyfold by increasing your tolerance for disorder, ambiguity, and tension. Often you do not need to know why you are anxious, only that you are. When a meeting falls into confusion, the urge to retreat or fix it immediately can be irresistible. Don't panic. You will help yourself immeasurably by hanging in despite your queasy feelings. If you wait just a while longer, you can help people find greater clarity and move in new directions.

WHAT DO YOU DO?

If you run meetings, you get a lot of anxiety, yours and others'. Somebody does something so outrageous that tension rises to the breaking point. You feel a chill creep up your spine, invade your belly, and clutch your throat. The room grows as quiet as Death Valley. Everyone waits for you to fix it. Whatever action you take, there is always a group expert waiting to tell you what you should have done. The loudest person will soon insist that this is not what "people" came for. Those most anxious of all, hoping caffeine will fix everything, want a break.

Surely, you think, there is something you could say that would make it all OK. Groups expect you to be an inspiring leader, a take-charge manager, and a supportive facilitator. They project fantasies on you—of parents, teachers, bosses, cops, and con artists. If you lead the meeting, you must know what to do.

How much of this do you expect of yourself? And how much of what you expect is based on what they expect? How can you learn to accept whatever you feel and carry on with constructive intent? How do you learn to reduce your own anxiety in tense situations? This chapter will help you answer these questions. If you can't avoid the anxious part of yourself, why not make your feelings work for you? As you succeed, you will find the capability for managing yourself in such a way that the groups you lead will do more while you do less. You will relieve yourself of a long list of shoulds, oughts, and have-to-do's that sap your energy, bog you down, stress you out, and hold others back.

Here are the perspectives on managing anxiety that we have found most useful.

1. VISIT THE "FOUR ROOMS OF CHANGE"

Perhaps the simplest way to understand our point of view about anxiety is to spend a few minutes in our favorite virtual dwelling place, Claes Janssen's (2005) "four rooms of change." Janssen, a Swedish social psychologist, made an inspired leap in the 1970s. He devised a model of human development you can learn quickly if you are willing to reflect on your own experience.

For decades we have presented the following diagram at the start of interactive meetings. We have found it a great anxiety reducer for people to know that we do not know how to avoid anxiety and in any case consider it an important milestone on the road to purposeful action. Moreover, Janssen's model helps us manage our own anxiety. As we have worked with it over the years, we have come to appreciate all of the rooms.

First, let us describe the rooms as we experience them. Then we will tell you how we introduce this model in meetings. Start in the Contentment Room, where everything is fine, the world secure, soft lights, music, and easy chairs. Why would we change anything? Pause. ... Breathe deeply. ... Relax. ...

But then something happens! A thunderstorm. An earthquake. We interrupt this music to bring you a breaking story: fires and floods coming your way. We are inundated with messages we would rather not hear, overwhelmed with information we cannot absorb. We seek refuge. And the nearest way out is through the door marked Denial.

In the Denial Room, we hunker down on a hard bench in the corner. The room is windowless, the air heavy and hard to breathe. We sit on our feelings. We smile with tight lips. Deep down we sense that all is not right. It's better not to

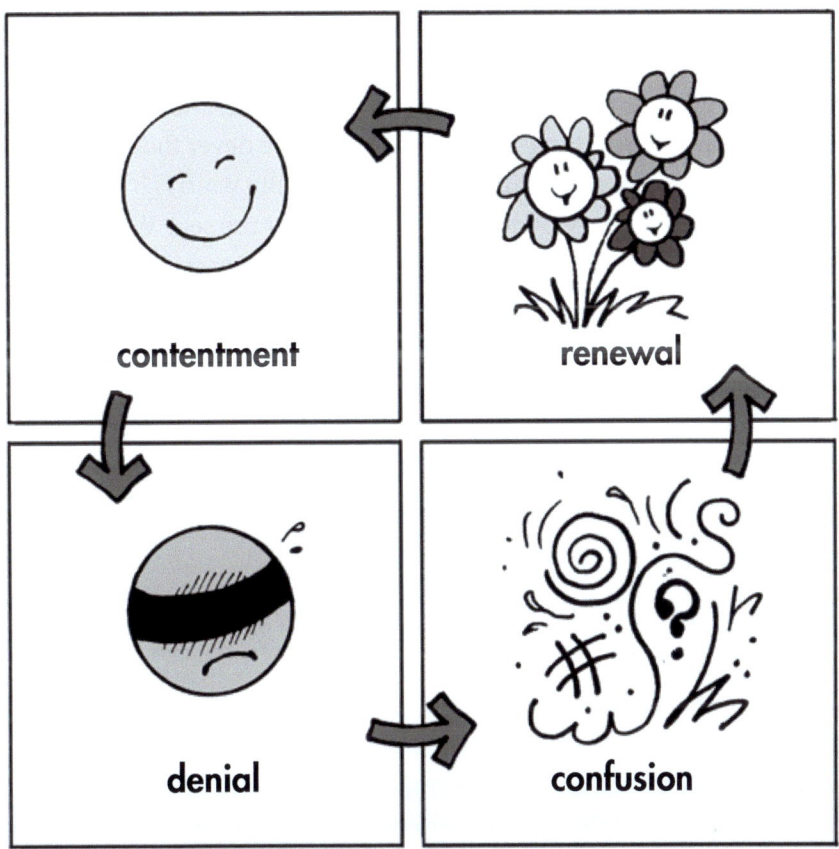

know. So we act as if nothing is happening. After a time, we may connect with some buried part of ourselves. We do not like this place. We are angry for having got into it. In fact, we're overwhelmed with feelings—fear, apprehension, excitement, and above all the urge to move.

Suddenly we look around and realize that in our agitation we have fled Denial and gone through the door marked Confusion. Anxiety is the décor of the Confusion Room. Bright lights flash the colors of the spectrum. Music, sometimes louder than we can stand or softer than we can hear, stops and starts at random. We see walls covered with writing we can't decipher.

We search for a way out. No exit strategy seems obvious. There are several doors. Access to any one of them requires that we make sense out of chaotic images that boggle our brains, agitate our bodies, and deplete our spirits. Unlike the Denial Room, though, now we have a lot to work with. We are aware that we want out. We know that we feel frustrated. As we struggle for clarity, new patterns emerge, possibilities we never considered until now.

Little by little, without our pushing on them, doors to the Renewal Room start popping open. Then, in a few moments more, everything becomes possible. We choose a door and emerge into bright sunshine, fresh air, and a stimulating breeze. Roads beckon, lined with things to do and see that we never thought could be ours.

In the Renewal Room, everything seems possible. But wait! Is it? We must choose. Will we pick the city or the woods? The mountains or the sea? We cannot be in two places at once. We settle for a path that attracts us, turning our back on all others. In no time we have walked ourselves back into Contentment, albeit with a new sense of purpose. To be in Contentment may be the most satisfying and productive room of all. In the words of Bengt Lindstrom, who has worked with this model for years, "In Contentment we harvest the fruits of the seeds planted in Renewal. We ought to make the seasons of Renewal and Contentment last as long as we can. We cannot avoid Denial and Confusion, but we can make them less fearful."

2. LET THE FOUR ROOMS WORK FOR YOU

There you have the story we tell ourselves. None of this do we say in meetings. However, one way we manage our own anxiety is to introduce people at the start to the possibility that things may not go smoothly all the time. We use a much leaner tale to describe what people might experience, referring them to the chart presented earlier.

For example, in Contentment (we tell the group), we're happy with the status quo and don't need to change anything. However, stuff happens. When struck by turbulent circumstances, such as information we'd rather not have, Denial is a normal retreat, a room to pass through but not live in. (If you confront people in Denial, they will deny it.) When we acknowledge that we don't like where we are, we move ourselves into Confusion. This is the room of uncertainty and high anxiety. It is also the room of possibility, for we now are looking full-time for a way out. As we confront the mess and confusion, we begin to see patterns not visible before. As we move toward creative solutions, we find ourselves in the Renewal Room.

We point out that people in this meeting could live in any room at any moment. We have known groups to move quickly from room to room as they deal with a sea of information. We also are not surprised that groups spend time in Denial and Confusion before moving into Renewal and Contentment.

Nor are we shocked when, on rare occasions, people freeze in place for what seems like an eternity. We tell people we are not predicting what they will do or requiring that they do anything. We're describing what could happen. We know that people would prefer that we, as leaders, keep everybody in Contentment or

Renewal. Alas, we say, we don't know how to do that! We accept all the rooms as possibilities when you do purposeful work. We end our briefing with the hope that group members will do the same. Over the years, we have repeatedly heard people refer to the four rooms during a meeting, making legitimate their feelings, especially when things get rough. This structure makes things easier for everybody and helps us keep ourselves centered.

3. EXPERIENCE THE BENEFITS OF CONFUSION

Now, here is what we do not say. Based on decades of experience, we believe that the Confusion Room, the décor of which is high anxiety, provides the most useful space in which to work when Renewal is your goal. In Contentment nobody needs to do anything. In Denial nobody wants to do anything. The apathy and lack of energy debilitates people. In Confusion everybody wants out. That is the place where leadership can make a big difference. Nobody likes Confusion, but in the middle of a tense meeting Confusion is not a bad place to be. Why would we consider it functional to live in a space no one likes? A physical/emotional state that some people take drugs to relieve? Well, we are not talking about clinical anxiety, that unfocused, nameless dread that overcomes many of us now and then and a few of us all of the time. We are talking about commonplace anxious meetings in a diverse world of nonstop change, when people wonder whether they will agree on a goal, be heard, solve the problem, make the decision, fashion the plan, cooperate, learn, and still make it home for dinner. In short, the Confusion Room has many doors. One leads back to Denial. The others welcome you to Renewal. Anxiety represents energy looking for a constructive outlet.

TEN WAYS TO MANAGE ANXIETY

There are simple ways to manage both a group's anxiety and your own. None require special training. All, however, take self-knowledge, patience, and the capacity to contain your feelings without acting them out. In short meetings of a day or less, a group may go in and out of the Confusion Room in minutes or hours. During meetings of 2 or 3 days, we are not surprised when people say they are confused for an extended period. It may not be much clock time, but it feels like a lifetime when you lead the meeting!

We base our coping strategies on the premise that a group will convert meeting-induced anxiety into excitement if you are patient. We offer you 10 ways to do that. When you feel secure using one, certify yourself as competent, and move to the next. After adding six of the 10 to your repertoire, give yourself a Certificate of Completion in Basic Anxiety Management (CCBAM). Or send us an email saying what you did, and we'll award you one.

1. USE THE FOUR ROOMS OF CHANGE IN MEETINGS

You need only 2 or 3 minutes to introduce this concept at the start of a meeting. When people know that you accept everything and everyone, they are more likely to accept everything and everybody, too. Hearing that you don't know how to avoid denial and confusion—indeed, that you consider both as normal—makes it easier for others to do the same. Moreover, you no longer need to worry about either state. Over the past decades, we have heard people say dozens of times, "Guess we've been in denial about that until now." Or, "I'm living in the Confusion Room." Such insights made public go a long way toward keeping groups whole. If they stay whole, they keep working.

2. JUST STAND THERE AND . . . BREATHE

A natural tendency when anxious is to hold your breath. We may do that any time we are faced with stressful problems, difficult people, or intractable conflicts. Holding the breath increases the stress. Your palms sweat, muscles tense, and you feel jumpy or nauseous. Breathing relieves a lot. Taking two or three deep breaths is a helpful way to lessen the symptoms. There will be a moment in the near future where you have to make a decision and have no idea what to do. Here's something to try:

- Just stand there. Contain your feelings.

- Be aware of your agitation, your fear that things are getting out of hand, your impulse to fix it fast.

- Wait. Look around.

- Exhale as much air as you can.

- Take a big, deep breath.

- Hold it a few seconds.

- Repeat as needed, until somebody says what needs saying.

Try it. You'll be amazed at what you can do by exchanging the CO_2 in your lungs for oxygen. It's the greatest source of free energy on planet Earth. Be sure to tank up the next time you become anxious.

3. CHECK YOUR NEGATIVE PREDICTIONS

Negative predictions are often the cause of a great deal of anxiety. These are thoughts not of what's really happening but of what could go wrong. You jump into the future, thinking, "This is going to fall apart," "I can't pull it off," "The group is going to blame me," or "I'm going to fail." You feel as bad as if your prediction had already come true. While the scenario isn't real, the feelings are.

What to do? First, check your own thoughts. Are you making a negative prediction? If yes, pull yourself back by thinking, "It hasn't happened yet." Group members may have similar apprehensions. You have the advantage of knowing that if you wait, stay engaged, and keep alert, the situation will clarify. We believe the best way to approach such situations is with curiosity. What will this group do? Remember, you can always act, change direction, or call a break. The fact that you wait 30 seconds does not limit your options. You'll feel relieved, and the group won't even notice.

4. TRACK YOUR INNER DIALOGUE

To follow our own streams of consciousness while leading meetings is to explore an underground river so vast it is a wonder how we navigate it. It's amazing how often we fall into mind reading, imagining others' motives and attitudes.

What about that woman who's working her Palm Pilot under the table? Why did she come? Maybe she doesn't want to be here. I could ask her. But that might embarrass her. Maybe nobody wants to be here. I've heard that people in this place [profession, industry, age group] don't have much patience. They just want solutions fast. I'll never meet their expectations. What do they really want? If I knew, could I supply it?

Our inner dialogue never stops. We worry that we're moving too fast or too slow. We wonder what the quiet people think. We worry about having too much information or not enough. We wonder if we *really* have the right people, given what they are saying and doing. If a group could hear played over a loudspeaker what goes through our heads as we lead them, they might be vastly entertained. They would be unlikely to do any work.

Of course, ours is not the only inner dialogue. Add one for every person in the room. Consider it normal. Contain your anxiety. Recognize it, accept it, and consider it part of your job. Are you reacting to something in the room, or just what's in your head? Give yourself a reality check. Stay open to possibilities.

5. EXPERIMENT WITH SILENCE

In our facilitation workshops, we sometimes ask people to stand up, close their eyes, and imagine leading a group. We have them say out loud, "Does anyone have anything to add?" Their imaginary group says nothing. They are to stand in silence, eyes closed, and to raise a hand when they feel they must say something. In every group the first hand goes up in about 6 seconds. In 20 seconds, a quarter of the group have raised their hands. About 90 percent of hands go up within a minute. A few people, however, will stand mute until their legs buckle. If you are among them, you can skip this practice tip.

If you are not, here's your homework for your next meeting. When a group falls silent, pause and notice the moment you feel you must speak. Could you just stand there quietly and wait for 20, 30, 40 seconds more? Of course you couldn't. Thirty seconds is two lifetimes. But you don't have to endure such agony. Just try holding your tongue while counting slowly to 10. It will seem like an hour. However, you will do no damage to the group. You might, just might, leave enough space for someone to say something that could change everything.

Fortunately, somebody in every meeting knows what to say. You can only learn that if you wait long enough for them to say it. (If you try it, let us know what happens.) We keep the door open by listening without acting. We are mindful that each time we break the silence, we deprive someone of a chance to make a valuable observation. If we treat silence as a problem to be solved, we deprive others of a chance to take care of themselves. Just waiting often is all a group needs from us to shift toward active dialogue, reality checking, and creative collaboration.

6. GET PEOPLE MOVING

Nothing relieves anxiety better than physical movement. When people want to run from the task, that's the perfect time to invite them to get up—and keep working. In large-group meetings, we look for opportunities to let people move. It is natural for people to move when breaking into small groups. We ask people to post their own flipcharts. We solicit their help in taking notes, leading conversations, summarizing what they hear. It is natural for people to move if they need a break. We suggest that people who need a break take it at any time. They need not wait until midmorning or midafternoon. (If your mind is on personal needs, you can't focus on the agenda, anyway.)

When a meeting offers places for people to walk outside, we may ask a group if they want to take a longer lunch or take a short walk during afternoon break. We know of colleagues who combine movement with work by asking people to pair up, take a walk outside the room, and talk over an issue of concern to the group.

7. STATE THE OBVIOUS

The legendary Gestalt therapist Frederick S. Perls once stopped suddenly during a public lecture after several provocative comments. "Right now," he said, "I have nothing to communicate." He fell silent. There was a long pause, filled, said the meeting transcript, by "uneasy, random laughter." Perls (1957) waited several seconds. "Now," he said at last, "you see what I just did was a typical little piece of Gestalt therapy. I just expressed what I felt, and through this expression I managed to go on. I reestablished contact. I felt a warm laughter. I felt that you were with me at this moment. I was able to finish this unpleasant situation, this bit of discomfort that I and maybe you felt, when I became silent."

When you state the obvious, you signal your presence. You take care of yourself. Here are some phrases we have used over the years:

- "There are many opinions on this. Do we have them all?"

- "We've spent a long time on this topic. Is there more to say, or can we move on?"

- "I don't know about you, but I'm ready for a break."

- "Clearly, this issue stirs up strong feelings."

- "I'm confused about how this conversation relates to our purpose."

- "At this moment I haven't the foggiest idea what to do."

- Anytime you state the obvious, wait 5 or 10 seconds for a reaction.

8. CONSULT THE GROUP

Now and then we find ourselves leading groups with no idea what is going on and no idea what to do. Our strategy in these situations is to just wait. Nearly always somebody knows what to do. When nobody knows what to do, including us, we use our best tool of all. We stop meetings that are going nowhere and ask people what they want to do. Fortunately, we make this move rarely. It's reassuring to know we can do it, though. Try this in your next meeting when nothing is happening. Just say, "Hold it. We don't have to keep doing this." Then go around and ask each person who wants to speak to say whether he or she wishes to continue the meeting.

9. GROW YOURSELF BY LISTENING TO WHAT YOU'D RATHER NOT HEAR

In each meeting, we seek to stretch our capacity for tolerating statements we don't believe, ideas we oppose, and interaction styles that make us cringe. We stay aware of our internal tug of war between our own and others' concepts of right and wrong, truth and falsity, valid information, and what ordinary words mean. As we experience our potential for negative predictions, mind reading, stereotyping, mistrust, and anxiety, we find it easier to accept that this is where groups usually start.

The more we learn to live with uncertainty and remain curious about what's to come, the better prepared we are to value each group's struggle. So we resist the tendency to manage our own anxiety by talking, asking questions, explaining, repeating, or changing the subject. When we're not sure what to do, we don't do anything.

The more we learn to hear all views without reacting, the more a group is likely to express all sides of polarized issues. We train ourselves to listen for the parts of each statement with which we agree. We counteract our tendency to make a case (inside our heads, of course) for the parts we oppose. To the extent we act congruent with our philosophy that all statements contain value, the easier we make it for task groups to do the same.

10. KNOW WHY YOU ARE THERE

One way we manage our own anxiety is to remind ourselves before every meeting that what we are doing matters. We believe that we live our values in every meeting and find we need to align ourselves with the goals. What larger purposes are served by our presence? So much is going on during a meeting, we need to anchor ourselves in the meaning of this gathering if we are to know when to stand still and when to act. Larry Dressler put this issue eloquently while reading a draft of this chapter: "I spend quiet time before every meeting asking myself, 'What am I here to contribute? What are the central ideas on which I don't compromise?' If I know my 'center' in these matters, I can easily access it when I'm standing in the fire of anxiety, conflict, and confusion."

After some particularly tough moments leading a meeting, our colleague Grace Potts summed up her experience with anxiety in the form of advice to herself:

- "Process is more important than content.

- "Don't get distracted with last-minute panic attacks. I was so sucked into the panic over disruptive people, I missed a gaping error in the agenda. There was no time planned for moving from small groups back into the large group. It took sacrificing a break and some negotiating to end on time and finish everything.

- "Repeat the goals. Repeat the goals. Repeat the goals.

- "Repeat the ground rules. Repeat the ground rules. Repeat the ground rules.

- "You're really not in control of anything."

How did the meeting come out, Grace?
"All in all, it was excellent. We ended on time and met all our goals for the day. We even met a few goals we didn't know we had."

PRINCIPLE 7: IN SUMMARY

Learn to accept anxiety as an inevitable traveling companion when the stakes are high, issues complicated, perceptions diverse, and answers uncertain. You can grow your capacity for leadership by increasing your tolerance for such natural conditions as disorder, ambiguity, and uncertainty.

SUGGESTIONS FOR YOUR NEXT MEETING

To make friends with anxiety, try one or more of these:

- Present the four rooms of change on a flipchart at the start.

- When things get sticky, consciously take two or three deep breaths. Notice whether you are making a negative prediction. If so, come back to the present.

- Look for a chance to stand in silence for 10 or 15 seconds, and see whether anybody fills it.

- Arrange for people to move if they've been sitting for a long time.

- If unsure of what to do next, try consulting the group.

BIBLIOGRAPHY

Ackoff, R. L. (1974). *Redesigning the future: A systems approach to societal problems.* New York: Wiley.
Agazarian, Yvonne M. (1997). *Systems-centered theory for groups.* New York: Guilford Press.
Agazarian, Yvonne M., & Sandra Janoff. (1993). Systems theory in small groups. In H. Kaplan & B. Sadock (Eds.), *Comprehensive textbook of group psychotherapy.* Baltimore: Williams & Wilkins.
Asch, Solomon. (1952). *Social psychology.* New York: Prentice Hall.
Auden, W. H. (1947). *The age of anxiety: A baroque ecologue.* New York: Random House.
Bion, Wilfred. (1961). *Experience in groups.* London: Tavistock.
Brown, Juanita, & David Isaacs. (2005). *World café.* Berrett-Koehler.
Bushe, Gervase R. (1995, Fall). Advances in appreciative inquiry as an organization development intervention. *Organization Development Journal, 13*(3), 14–22.
Buzan, Tony. (1991). *Use both sides of your brain: New mind-mapping techniques* (3rd ed.). New York: Plume Books.

Cresswell, Julie. (2006, December 17). How suite it isn't: A dearth of female bosses. *New York Times*, Business, 1, 9–10.

Emery, Fred E., & Eric L. Trist. (1973). *Toward a social ecology*. New York: Plenum.

Faucheux, Claude. (1984, October 10–13). Leadership, power and influence within social systems. Paper prepared for a "Symposium on the Functioning of the Executive," Case Western University, Cleveland, OH.

FutureSearching, the Newsletter of the Future Search Network. Available: www.futuresearch.net.

Janssen, Claus. (2005). *The four rooms of change* (Förändringens fyra rum). Stockholm: Ander & Lindstrom. (An English version of the book is available online at www.claesjanssen.com/ books. For training in its use as a change management tool, see www.andolin.com/fourrooms.)

Lawrence, Paul R., & Jay W. Lorsch. (1967a, November–December). New management job: The integrator. *Harvard Business Review*.

Lawrence, Paul R., & Jay W. Lorsch. (1967b). *Organization and environment: Managing differentiation and integration*. Boston: Harvard Business School Press.

Lewin, Kurt. (1948). *Resolving social conflicts*. Edited by Gertrude W. Lewin. New York: Harper & Row.

Lewin, Kurt, Ronald Lippitt, & Ralph White. (1939). Patterns of aggressive behaviour in experimentally created "social climates." *Journal of Social Psychology, 10*, 271–99.

Lippitt, Lawrence L. (1998). *Preferred futuring: Envision the future you want and unleash the energy to get there*. San Francisco: Berrett-Koehler.

Madsen, Benedicte, & Søren Willert. (2006). *Working on boundaries: Gunnar Hjelholt and applied social psychology*. Aarhus, Denmark: Aarhus University Press.

Meade, Chris. (2006, October 1). Meeting research study summary. Available: www.studergroup.com/dotCMS/knowledgeAssetDetail?inode=269049.

Merrill, Alexandra. (1991). *Self-differentiation: A day with John and Joyce Weir* (three-video set). Philadelphia: Blue Sky Productions.

Mix, Philip J. (2006, September). A monumental legacy: The unique and unheralded contributions of John and Joyce Weir to the human development field. *Journal of Applied Behavioral Science, 42*(3), 276–99.

Owen, Harrison. (1997). *Open space technology: A user's guide*. San Francisco: Berrett-Koehler.

Perls, Frederick S. (1957, March 6). Finding self through gestalt therapy. Cooper Union Forum Lecture Series: *The Self*. Available: www.gestalt.org/self.htm.

Rogelberg, S. G., D. J. Leach, P. B. Warr, & J. L. Burnfield. (2006). "Not another meeting!" Are meeting time demands related to employee well-being? *Journal of Applied Psychology, 91*(1), 83–96.

Schweitz, Rita, & Kim Martens (Eds.). (1995). *Future Search in school district change*. Lanham, MD: Rowman & Littlefield.

Weir, John. (1975). The personal growth laboratory. In K. Benne, L. P. Bradford, J. R. Gibb, & R. D. Lippitt (Eds.), *The laboratory method of changing and learning: Theory and application*. Palo Alto, CA: Science and Behavior Books.

Weisbord, Marvin R. (1987). *Productive workplaces: Organizing and managing for dignity, meaning and community*. Jossey-Bass, San Francisco.

Weisbord, Marvin R., & 35 Coauthors. (1992). *Discovering common ground*. San Francisco: Berrett-Koehler.

Weisbord, Marvin R. (2004). *Productive workplaces revisited: Dignity, meaning and community in the 21st century*. San Francisco: Jossey-Bass/Wiley.

Weisbord, Marvin, & Sandra Janoff. (2000). *Future Search: An action guide to finding common ground in organizations and communities* (2nd ed.). San Francisco: Berrett-Koehler.

Weisbord, Marvin, & Sandra Janoff. (2005). Faster, shorter, cheaper may be simple; it's never easy. *Journal of Applied Behavioral Science, 41*(1), 70–82.

Weisbord, Marvin, & Sandra Janoff. (2006). Clearing the air: The FAA's historic growth without gridlock conference. In B. Bunker & B. Alban (Eds.), *The handbook of large group methods: Creating systemic change in organizations and communities.* San Francisco: Jossey-Bass.

CHAPTER SUMMARY

Important parts of this chapter:

- Janssen's 1970 "4 Rooms of Change" model

- Ten ways to manage anxiety

- Realize that anxiety is inevitable

Anxiety need not be a hindrance to your public speaking exploits. Acknowledging anxiety, focusing it, and overcoming it can be a boon to your personal and career success. Janssen's model of anxiety, the "4 Rooms of Change" model, states that anxiety comes in four stages: contentment, denial, confusion, and finally, renewal. As a leader and speaker, you can lead your audience through these stages using the "Ten Ways to Manage Anxiety": 1) use the "4 Rooms of Change" model, 2) just stand there and breathe, 3) check your negative predictions, 4) track your inner dialogue, 5) experiment with silence, 6) get people moving, 7) state the obvious, 8) consult the group, 9) grow together by listening to what you'd rather not hear, and 10) know why you are there.

Lastly, be mindful that anxiety is inevitable, and it is largely up to you to dictate its effects upon you. It is up to you to learn about your body and mind, how and what things seem to bother you most, and how you can overcome these stressors. How nervousness and stress affect the body from a biological perspective is the topic of chapter 3.

CHAPTER 3
THE BIOLOGY OF NERVOUSNESS

In the reading from chapter 3, "The Consequences of Stress," you will learn about the biology of stress and nervousness. This biology spans the breadth of the human body and its various systems. This information is important because by knowing what is going on in your body, you can learn to deal with anxiety and its various manifestations. Bear in mind that your body needs an outlet for stress and anxiety. This chapter also includes information about various outlets for anxiety and stress.

THE CONSEQUENCES OF STRESS

by Jolynn Gardner

After reading this chapter, you will be able to:

- Provide a brief overview of the human nervous system.

- Explain the responses of the nervous and endocrine systems when stress is perceived.

- Identify short-term physiological and psychological effects that occur after stress has been perceived.

- Discuss the stress—illness connection regarding cardiovascular disease, immunosuppression, muscle tension, and other physical health issues.

- Explain the impact stress may have on psychological health, interpersonal relationships, organizational issues, and societal matters.

- Analyze how social disparities may influence the experience of stress among various population groups.

- Articulate the meaning of "stress proliferation" and recommend policy initiatives that may help address disparities in the experience of stress.

Jolynn Gardner, "The Consequences of Stress," *From Stress to Strength: Increasing Optimism, Gratitude, and Resiliency*, pp. 19-34. Copyright © 2015 by Cognella, Inc. Reprinted with permission.

You've heard this before ... stress can make you sick. This is most certainly true. It's also true, though, that stress is a natural part of life, and the stress response is necessary and vital to well-being. So, why does stress make us sick? As we've discussed [...], when stress is experienced too frequently, too intensely, or disproportionately, the toll on our bodies and minds can become overwhelming. Thus, stress has been linked to cardiovascular disease, headaches, anxiety, sleep disorders, memory issues, back pain, and a whole host of other issues. The explanation for this connection actually goes back to the stress response itself. To understand the connection between stress and disease, we have to start with the basics of the body's reaction to stress. (This is actually fascinating stuff. And it's important that we understand the mechanisms by which stress can harm us so that we can address them successfully.)

A VERY BASIC REVIEW

So, you probably remember from Biology class that the nervous system can be divided into two parts: the central nervous system and the peripheral nervous system. The central nervous system consists of the brain and spinal cord. The brain acts, of course, as "command central." Much of how we perceive and respond to stress is determined by the brain. More on that later. The spinal cord descends through your vertebrae and is the vital connection between the nerves in the rest of your body and your brain. Think of it as an "information highway" with traffic going to and coming from the brain (Figure 3.1).

The primary function of the peripheral nervous system is to connect the central nervous system with the organs, limbs, muscles, and other tissues of the body. The PNS also provides the interface with our environment via our senses and peripheral nerves (Jasmin, 2011). The PNS is divided into two parts: the somatic nervous system and the autonomic nervous system. The somatic system controls all of those actions and reactions that require *voluntary* control like muscle movement, walking, lifting your arm, and driving a car. The autonomic nervous system is that part of the peripheral nervous system that governs *involuntary* functions of heart beat, respiration, temperature regulation, digestion, hormone production, etc. Both the somatic and autonomic nervous systems can be affected by the perception of stress.

The communication between the PNS and the CNS occurs in an amazing fashion. Consider this example: You're cooking dinner, and you absentmindedly start to lower your hand onto a hot burner on your stove. In a nanosecond, the nerves in your hand sense the intense heat and convey that message via the PNS to the spinal cord and eventually the brain. Then, the brain synthesizes that information and deduces that touching the hot stove might not be a great idea. Then, it sends a message ("Don't touch that!") back through the spinal cord and the PNS to the voluntary muscles of the arm and you jerk your arm out of the way just before you touch your hand to the hot burner. Wow! Incredible. And, as mentioned, all of this happens in a split second—and we hardly ever pause to think about how amazing this is.

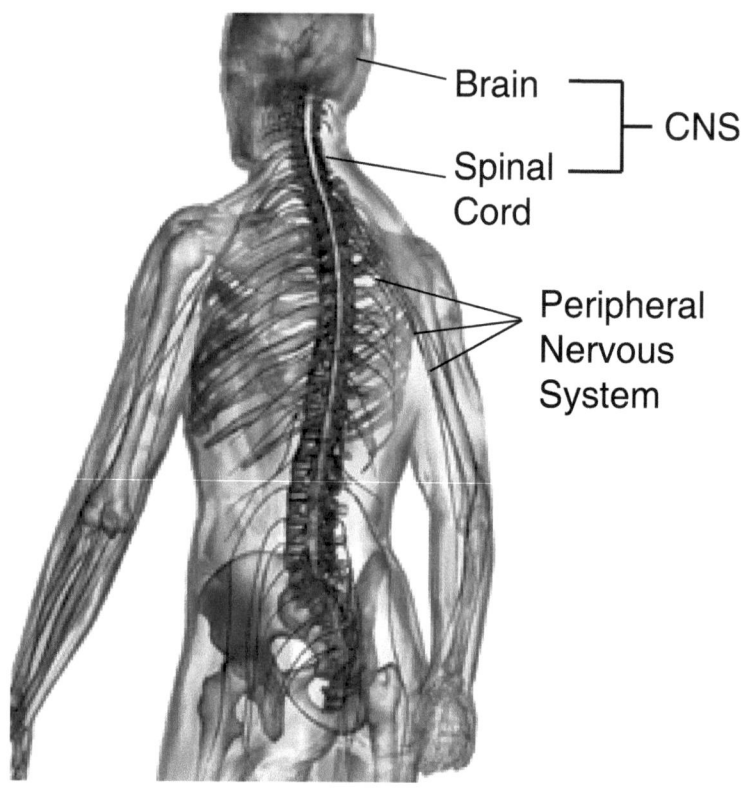

Figure 3.1 The Central and Peripheral Nervous Systems
Copyright © 2013 by User:BruceBlaus / Wikimedia Commons / CC BY 3.0.

The autonomic branch of the PNS is further divided into two more subsystems: the sympathetic nervous system and the parasympathetic nervous system. The sympathetic system becomes aroused when we either consciously or unconsciously perceive stress. In the hot stove example, the sympathetic branch of the autonomic nervous system was engaged. This causes us to be able to react quickly to stimuli. Our heart rate, blood pressure, respiration rate, and muscle tension all increase when the sympathetic branch of the autonomic nervous system is engaged. In other words, it's responsible for that fight-or-flight response.

The opposite of the sympathetic branch of the autonomic nervous system is the parasympathetic nervous system. The parasympathetic system induces the relaxation response, which is the opposite of the fight-or-flight response. When the parasympathetic system is activated, your biological responses slow down. Breathing and heart rate slow, muscles become less tense, and relaxation ensues. It is interesting to note that we actually have much more control over these autonomic systems than we realize. We can deliberately activate the sympathetic branch by worrying excessively or thinking pessimistically about something. Likewise, however, we can activate the parasympathetic system by practicing deep-breathing exercises, meditating, or doing something else to calm ourselves.

WHEN STRESS IS PERCEIVED …

Both the CNS and the PNS are involved in the perception of and reaction to stress. The perception of stress occurs in the *cerebral cortex* of the brain. The cerebral cortex is the "thinking" portion of your brain. It becomes more aware and functions at a higher level when stress is perceived. Emotions are also involved in the stress response. The *limbic system* (also a part of the brain) responds to the perception of stress as well and largely determines how you "feel" about a given stressor. The arousal of the cerebral cortex and limbic system then leads to stimulation of the *hypothalamus*. The hypothalamus is the part of the brain that produces hormones that control body temperature, moods, and release of other hormones from glands in the body (Hadley and Levine, 2007).

The hypothalamus activates the sympathetic branch of the autonomic nervous system. This, then, leads to the stimulation of the *adrenal medulla*. The adrenal glands are located on top of each kidney. The medulla is the outside part of the gland. The adrenal medulla releases two hormones: adrenaline and noradrenaline. Adrenaline causes the following bodily responses:

- Glucose is released into the bloodstream (to serve as a ready source of energy for fighting or fleeing);

- Major arteries dilate or open up (to facilitate faster delivery of blood, oxygen, and nutrients to organs and tissues during fighting or fleeing);

- Heart rate and stroke volume increase (again, to facilitate efficient delivery of blood, oxygen, and nutrients to organs and tissues);

- Metabolic rate and respiration rate increase (metabolic rate increases to improve energy synthesis, while respiration rate increases to provide more oxygen to the system).

Noradrenaline is responsible for:

- An increase in fatty acids being released into the bloodstream (also for energy);

- An increase in heart rate and blood pressure (to increase efficiency of nutrient and oxygen transport);

- A constriction of peripheral blood vessels (reducing blood flow to organs and tissues not essential in responding to stress);

- A temporary boost of immune activity via stimulation of white blood cells (to combat any attacks on the immunity of the body) (Dhabhar, 2009).

In addition to stimulating the adrenal medulla through activation of the sympathetic nervous system, the hypothalamus also stimulates the *pituitary gland*. The pituitary gland is located in the middle of the base of the brain and it controls several important functions in the body. During the stress response, the pituitary gland has three primary effects:

- It stimulates the *thyroid gland*, which results in an increase in the body's metabolic rate (to improve energy synthesis).

- It stimulates the *adrenal cortex gland* (the middle of the adrenal gland) to release the hormone *cortisol*. Cortisol is then responsible for:

    - Stimulating the liver to produce more glucose for energy;

    - Causing fats and proteins to be released into the bloodstream for energy; and

    - Diverting blood flow to large muscle groups (to get ready to fight or flee) and away from the brain.

- It releases the hormones *oxytocin* and *vasopressin*. These hormones cause the kidneys to reduce urine production, which contributes to increases in blood volume and blood pressure.

Other bodily responses to the perception of stress include the bracing and tensing of muscles as they prepare for action and a change in the rate of contractions in the intestinal tract (peristalsis).

So, a review of stress response tells us that the following effects occur when a person perceives stress:

- Heart rate increases

- Blood pressure increases

- Stroke volume increases

- Respiration rate increases

- Metabolic rate increases

- Glucose, fatty acid, and protein concentrations in the blood increase

- Major arteries dilate

- Peripheral blood vessels constrict

- Immune response temporarily increases

- Urine output decreases

- Muscles tense

- Rate of intestinal contractions changes

(Note: Review the preceding information and ask yourself if you are now starting to see the connections between stress and various illnesses.)

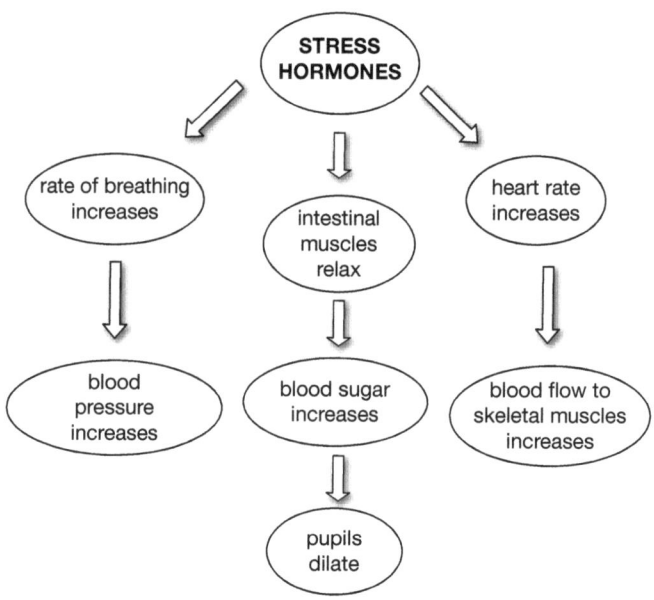

THE STRESS/ILLNESS CONNECTION

It is important to note once again that the stress response is a natural, necessary, and important reaction of the body to threats and challenges. It allows us to respond to danger in a timely and efficient fashion, which is obviously good—and, in some cases, life-saving. However, as stated earlier in this text, when the stress response is experienced too intensely or too often, it can contribute to illness. The previous discussion provides a basis for understanding these connections.

STRESS AND CARDIOVASCULAR DISEASE

One of the first illnesses to be linked to stress was cardiovascular disease. In 1978, the famous Framingham Heart Study first linked psychosocial factors to heart disease (Arruda, 2013). The connections now seem obvious. When we are stressed, several responses occur that tax our cardiovascular system: increases in heart rate, blood pressure, stroke volume, and amounts of glucose and fat entering the bloodstream, and constriction of some peripheral blood vessels. These responses are all positive and helpful when dealing with short-term stressors, but if they may be harmful to our cardiovascular system over the long term or if experienced too intensely.

Many of the cardiovascular concerns associated with stress can be traced to the promotion of *atherosclerosis* ("hardening of the arteries"). The National Heart, Lung, and Blood Institute provides a great description of atherosclerosis (2011):

> Atherosclerosis (ath-er-o-skler-O-sis) is a disease in which plaque (plak) builds up inside your arteries. Arteries are blood vessels that carry oxygen-rich blood to your heart and other parts of your body.
>
> Plaque is made up of fat, cholesterol, calcium, and other substances found in the blood. Over time, plaque hardens and narrows your arteries. This limits the flow of oxygen-rich blood to your organs and other parts of your body.
>
> Atherosclerosis can lead to serious problems, including heart attack, stroke, or even death.

So, how does stress relate to atherosclerosis? During the stress response, the body "dumps" extra fatty acids, cholesterol, glucose, and protein into the circulatory system as ready sources of energy. This can then lead to an acceleration of the accumulation of plaque, which, as stated previously, leads to atherosclerosis. The increase in blood pressure that also occurs during the stress response exacerbates this situation, creating additional strain on the heart and arteries.

Stress has been implicated as a causative factor in increasing other cardiovascular conditions as well. These include hypertension (elevated blood pressure) (Goldstein, 1983), high blood cholesterol levels (Friedman, Rosenman, and Carroll, 1958), and even sudden cardiac death (Engel, 1971). A *heart attack* occurs when blood and oxygen flow to the cardiac (heart) tissue is disrupted, either by a blockage in or a rupture of a coronary artery. A *stroke* occurs when blood and oxygen flow to the brain is interrupted. In both heart attacks and strokes, atherosclerosis and hypertension (high blood pressure) are potential contributing factors. Given that stress can contribute to these conditions, it can be rational, then, to conclude that stress may increase one's overall risk for cardiovascular disease. This seems logical, considering that when a person is stressed, his heart rate, stroke volume, and blood pressure increase, while at the same time, additional fat, glucose, and protein are being released into the circulatory system. As mentioned earlier, none of this is a concern when it occurs moderately and occasionally. However, if a person's stress response is in constant "overdrive" (due to perceptions, intensity of stressors, or other factors), the cardiovascular outcomes can be less than positive. If the person in question is also very sedentary or overweight or is a smoker, the negative effects can be even more pronounced. It's like a perfect storm of risk factors.

Finally, more recent studies have indicated that stress is a factor in obesity and, in particular, accumulation of abdominal fat (Mouchacca, Abbott, and Ball, 2013). Both obesity and high levels of abdominal fat have been identified as risk factors for cardiovascular disease.

STRESS AND IMMUNITY

Stress appears to have interesting effects on a person's immune response. As mentioned earlier, acute (short-term) stress appears to temporarily boost immune activity (Dhabhar, 2009). The body releases more white blood cells (leukocytes) to prepare for battle with potential invaders (bacteria, viruses, etc.). This increase in immune response generally lasts for 30 to 60 minutes, and then drops (Coe, 2010).

While acute short-term stress appears to lead to improvements in immune response, chronic stress often has the opposite effect. Stress over a longer period of time (lasting from days to months to years) has been shown to cause immunosuppression (Harrington, p. 117). Over time, exposure to chronic stress reduces immunity. This may be due partly to the effect of the hormone cortisol, which is elevated during times of stress and appears to also reduce the immune response (Cacioppo et al., 2002). Another possible explanation relates to the protein the body makes available for energy metabolism when under stress. Protein is a vital building block of *antibodies*, which are specialized immune-response cells designed to attack and destroy specific invaders. Use of protein as a source of energy during the stress response reduces the amount of protein available for antibody production. This, too, would impair the immune response over time.

STRESS AND MUSCLE TENSION

We've already mentioned that when a person perceives stress, the muscles in the body tense and get ready to fight or flee. So, it seems logical that musculoskeletal aches and pains could be logical outcomes of stress—especially chronic stress.

One common response to stress is called *bracing*. Most of us do this without even realizing it. Basically, our muscles tense and tighten, especially those in the back, shoulders, and neck. When a person experiences chronic stress or repeated bouts of acute stress, he or she may never completely relax these muscles. This can lead to a variety of effects, including neck pain, shoulder pain, backaches, and even headaches.

In fact, the most common type of headaches is a *tension-type headache*, which appears to be caused by bracing in the back, neck, and related muscle areas (Schafer, 1995).

OTHER EFFECTS OF STRESS ON HEALTH

While the connections between stress and other health conditions may not be as well researched or documented as the conditions already discussed, it is important to note that stress has been implicated as a contributing factor in a myriad of other health concerns. Current research may not conclusively prove that stress *causes* certain conditions, but it does provide evidence that stress indeed plays a role in exacerbating the following:

- Migraine headache pain (Hague, Rahman, Hogue, Hasan, Chowdhury, Khan, et al., 2012);

- Bruxism and temporomandibular pain (grinding of the teeth and jaw pain) (Franz, Giraki, Ommerborn, Raab, Schafer, Schneider, and Singh, 2010);

- Gastrointestinal disorders like irritable bowel disease (Khokar and Niazi, 2013);

- Allergic and asthmatic reactions (Mendez, Cairo, and Sant'Anna, 2013);

- Some cancers (Coleman, 2012; Levenson and Bemis, 1991);

- Autoimmune disorders like lupus and rheumatoid arthritis (Rosch, 2008);

- Memory impairment (Emdad and Sondergaard, 2006);

- Mental health disorders like depression and anxiety (Thoits, 2013; Hunt and Eisenberg, 2010; Eisenberg et al., 2009; Eisenberg et al., 2007);

- Incidences of self-injury (Gollust et al., 2008);

- Complicated grief syndrome (Schnider et al., 2007);

- Lower perceptions of quality of life (Hamaideh, 2013);

- Obesity and accumulation of abdominal fat (Mouchacca, Abbott, and Ball, 2013)

In general, the ways in which stress can contribute to illness can be summarized in four basic statements (Schafer, 1995):

1. Long-term wear and tear from excessive stress makes the body more susceptible to breakdown.
2. Acute emotional distress can precipitate physical ailments.
3. High stress can aggravate an existing illness.
4. Stress can result in behaviors (smoking, excessive drinking, unhealthy eating, etc.) that can lead to health issues.

Emotions	**Behavior**
irritability	smoking more
depression	restlessness
apprehension	drinking more
loss of confidence	loss of sex drive
alienation	loss of appetite
more fussy	accident prone
apathy	insomnia
Body	**Mind**
breathlessness	worrying
muscular twitches	muddled thinking
fatigue	impaired judgement
skin irritations	nightmares
frequent infections	indecisions
headaches	hasty decisions
taut muscles	negativity

(STRESS)

It must also be acknowledged here that a given stressful event does not *always* lead to illness. Other factors, such as coping resources, social support, and our environment also mediate this relationship. But, as Thoit stated in her 2010 review of stress research,

> When assessed more comprehensively, stress exposure has a much more substantial impact on the risks of psychological distress, depression, and other psychiatric disorders than researchers originally believed. Although comparable studies of combined stressors on physical health outcomes have not been done, similar findings are probable, given that hundreds of studies show that at least one type of stress (negative events) harms physical and mental health alike.

In other words, stress *can* make us sick. But the good news is that these effects of stress *can* be moderated and we *don't have to let it* make us sick. ☺ We have the power to influence and reduce the stress/illness correlation.

GOING BEYOND THE PERSONAL HEALTH IMPACT

Of course, stress has implications far beyond personal health. These effects are important and must be considered if we are to gain a full appreciation for the pervasiveness of stress.

INTERPERSONAL EFFECTS

The effects of stress on an interpersonal level are easily understood, mostly because virtually all of us have experienced them. Think about your own behavior towards others when you are feeling stressed ... are you more patient, less irritable, and generally more tolerant? Or, is the opposite more likely to be true? Stress often causes us to exhibit behavior that Schafer (1995) characterizes as the "AIAI" response: aggravation, irritation, anger, and impatience. In other words, stress really doesn't make a person all that pleasant. This, in turn, impacts his or her relationships. It's hard to be empathetic, considerate, tolerant, and compassionate when we are perceiving stress. If you need an example of this, simply observe people driving in rush hour traffic.

We tend to take our stress out on virtually all people with whom we're associated, even strangers. When stressed, we tend to smile less, we tend to be less tolerant, and we are much more likely to overlook the needs of others. No one in our lives bears the brunt of this, though, more than our family and close friends. This really isn't fair—or often justified—but it does happen, probably more often than we'd like. Thus, stress certainly has an impact on our relationships with others. We'll discuss ideas for remedying this in later chapters, but simply being aware of this tendency is often helpful in minimizing this effect.

ORGANIZATIONAL AND SOCIETAL EFFECTS

An impressive amount of stress research has been conducted in workplace settings and the results have certainly been eye-opening. Various studies have linked stress in the workplace to burnout, low productivity, increased absenteeism, increased health care costs, lower job satisfaction, and increased turnover (Posen, 2013). (Note: For college students, "low productivity" and "absenteeism" can often translate to lower grades and less-than-stellar academic achievements.) None of these effects is terribly positive for the employee or the employer. But, the fact that they are direct outcomes of perceptions of stress in the workplace seems logical. So, while there is ample evidence for *personal* stress management, there is also a need for *organizational change*. A full-fledged discussion of the tenets of effective workplace change is beyond the scope of this text, but the merits of it need to be acknowledged. Corporations and workplaces have a vested interest in helping employees reduce stress. Lower stress can translate to improved job satisfaction, lower absenteeism and healthcare costs, lower turnover, and improved productivity. Each one of these issues affects the bottom line of the workplace. Dare we say that a happier workplace just might be a more productive and possibly even more profitable workplace? The relationships among all of these variables are complex, but there are logical connections here. The benefits can be achieved through a variety of methods, starting with culture and workplace change, coupled with enhancement of personal coping resources.

It isn't difficult to make the leap from organizational effects of stress to societal effects. If increased perceptions of stress can have such negative effects in the workplace, they then likely produce many similar results in the larger society.

It's important to note, though, that exposure to stress is not equally distributed across society and this unequal distribution fosters inequalities in physical and psychological well-being (Thoit, 2010). It appears that females, young adults, members of racial-ethnic minority groups, divorced and widowed persons, and poor and working-class individuals experience significantly more chronic difficulties in their lives and face more cumulative burdens overall. They also report more negative health outcomes associated with stress, compared to other groups (Thoit, 2010). Racial and ethnic minority groups are exposed to significantly more discrimination stress than their white counterparts are, which additionally increases overall stress for these individuals (Thoit, 2010). Another factor compounding these effects is *stress proliferation*. Stress proliferation occurs when an initial stressor gives rise to additional stressors, thus complicating a person's experiences. Stress proliferation can occur over a life course and can also span generations. This effect might help explain why early life structural disadvantages may increase the likelihood of poor health outcomes over a life course (Thoit, 2010). When all of these factors are considered, it becomes clear that conquering stress effectively requires not only personal change, but organizational and societal initiative as well.

Thoit (2010) recommends three policy initiatives to address the disparities in the experience of stress:

> **Policy Implication 1:** To reduce the health impacts of major adversities in individuals' lives, coping and social support interventions that most effectively buffer the effects of stress should be identified, their best practices distilled, and their programs disseminated for wider use by community agencies, volunteer and religious organizations, and employers.
>
> **Policy Implication 2:** To reduce health inequalities, the structural conditions that put people "at risk of risks"—i.e., discrimination, poverty, residential segregation, inadequate schools, unemployment—should be the focus of ameliorative social programs and policies.
>
> **Policy Implication 3:** To reduce health disparities over the life course, policies and programs should target children who are at long-term health risk due to early exposure to poverty, inadequate schools, and stressful family circumstances.

As much as possible, it would be wise for each of us to do what we can to increase awareness of these issues and to work to address them. We must also acknowledge that each one of us has a stake in creating positive environments. And, perhaps that is where we each can make our greatest contribution to the reduction of stress. We have the ability to positively impact each and every situation we encounter—at work, at home, in college, and elsewhere (even the grocery store). Every little positive interaction makes a difference. To this end, learning to effectively cope with stress is not only a personal endeavor, but it is an *altruistic* endeavor as well in that it improves our interactions with others. This, in turn, can potentially reduce some of the organizational stress we all undoubtedly endure from time to time. We may not always be able to produce sweeping organizational or societal changes, but we can always seek to make our little corners of the world a bit brighter. It's the right thing to do—and, when we approach life with a bit more positive outlook, it just might be contagious to those around us.

SUMMARY

This chapter has focused on the consequences of stress. Hopefully, the discussion has fostered an understanding of not only the physical responses to stress, but also the psychological, behavioral, and social effects of stress. Gaining an appreciation for the potential consequences of stress can be enlightening. It can also provide motivation for exploring resources that might help you cope with stress more effectively.

REFERENCES

Arruda, H. (2013). "Research Milestones. Framingham Heart Study." www.framinghamheart-study.org. Retrieved September 9, 2013.

Bremmer, D. and Narayan, M. (1998). "The Effects of Stress on Memory and the Hippocampus Throughout the Lifecycle: Implications for Child Development and Aging." *Development and Psychopathology*, 10, 871–885.

Cacioppo, J., Kiecolt-Glaser, J., Malarkey, W., Laskowski, B., Rozlog, L., et al. (2002). "Autonomic and Glucocorticoid Associations with the Steady-State Expression of latent Epstein-Barr Virus." *Hormones and Behavior*, 42, 32–41.

Coe, C. (2010). "All Roads Lead to Psychoneuroimmunology." In J. M. Suls, K. W. Davidson, and R. M. Kaplan (Eds.), *Handbook of Health Psychology and Behavioral Medicine*, New York: The Guilford Press, 182–199.

Coleman, R. (2012). "Stress and Poor Cancer Outcomes: It's More Than Psychological." *OB/GYN Clinical Alert*, 29(7), 53–56.

Dhabhar, F. (2009). "Enhancing versus Suppressive Effects of Stress on Immune Function: Implication for Immunoprotection and Immunopathology." *Neuroimmunomodulation*, 16, 300–317.

Eisenberg, D., Golberstein, E., and Hunt, J. B. (2009) "Mental Health and Academic Success in College," *The B.E. Journal of Economic Analysis & Policy*, Vol. 9, Iss. 1 (Contributions), Article 40.

Eisenberg, D., Gollust, S. E., Golberstein, E., and Hefner, J. L. (2007). "Prevalence and Correlates of Depression, Anxiety and Suicidality Among University Students." *American Journal of Orthopsychiatry*, 77(4), 534-542.

Emdad, R. and Sondergaard, H. (2006). "General Intelligence and Short-Term Memory Impairments in Post-Traumatic Stress Disorder Patients." *Journal of Mental Health*, 15(2), 205–216.

Engel, G. (1971). "Sudden and Rapid Death During Psychological Stress: Folklore or Folk Wisdom?" *Annals of Internal Medicine*, 74, 771–782.

Franz, M., Giraki, M., Ommerborn, M., Raab, W., Schafer, R., Schneider, C., and Singh, P. (2010). "Correlation Between Stress, Stress-Coping and Current Sleep Bruxism." *Head and Face Medicine*, 6, 2–10.

Friedman, M., Roseman, R., and Carroll, V. (1958). "Changes in Serum Cholesterol and Blood-Clotting Time in Men Subjected to Cyclic Variation of Occupational Stress." *Circulation*, 17, 852–861.

Goldstein, D. (1983). "Plasma Catecholamines and Essential Hypertension: An Analytical Review." *Hypertension*, 5, 86–99.

Gollust, S., Eisenberg, D., and Golberstein, E. (2008). "Prevalence and Correlates of Self-Injury Among University Students." *Journal of American College Health*, 56(5), 491–498.

Hadley, M. E. and Levine, J. E. (2007). *Endocrinology*. 6th ed. Upper Saddle River, NJ: Pearson Prentice Hall, 111–133.

Hamaideh, S. (2012). "Occupational Stress, Social Support, and Quality of Life Among Jordanian Mental Health Nurses." *Issues in Mental Health Nursing*, 33(1), 15–23.

Haque, B., Rahman, K., Hoque, A., Hasan, A., Chowdhury, R., Khan, S., Alam, M., Habib, M., and Mohammad, Q. (2012). "Precipitating and Relieving Factors of Migraine versus Tension Type Headache." *BMC Neurology*, 12, 82.

Harrington, R. (2013). "Stress, Illness and the Immune System." In *Stress, Health, and Wellbeing*. Belmont, CA: Wadsworth Cengage Learning, 95–130.

Hunt, J. and Eisenberg, D. (2010). "Mental Health Problems and Help-Seeking Behavior Among College Students: A Narrative Review." *Journal of Adolescent Health*, 46(1), 3–10.

Jasmin, L. (2011). "MedlinePlus." US National Library of Medicine, National Institutes of Health. www.nlm.nih.gov. Retrieved September 9, 2013.

Khokhar, N. and Niazi, A. (2013). "A Long-Term Profile of Patients with Irritable Bowel Syndrome." *Journal of the College of Physicians and Surgeons Pakistan*, 23. 388–391.

Mendes, M., Cairo, S., and Sant'Anna, C. (2013). "Stress and Asthma During Childhood and Adolescence." *Clinical Practice*, 10, 641–647.

Mouchacca, J., Abbot, G., and Ball, K. (2013). "Associations Between Psychological Stress, Eating, Physical Activity, Sedentary Behaviours and Body Weight Among Women: A Longitudinal Study." *BMC Public Health*, 13, 828.

National Heart, Lung, and Blood Institute (2011). "What Is Atherosclerosis?" http://www.nhlbi.nih.gov/health/health-topics/topics/atherosclerosis/. Web. Retrieved Sept. 11, 2013.

Posen, D. (2013). *Is Work Killing You?* Toronto: House of Anasi Press.

Rosch, P. (2008). "Perplexing Immune Responses to Stress." *Health and Stress*, 9, 1–12.

Ross, S., Niebling, B., and Heckert, T. (1999). "Sources of Stress Among College Students." *College Student Journal*, Jun, Vol. 33 Issue 2, 312–318.

Schafer, W. (1995). *Stress Management for Wellness*. Harcourt-Brace Publishing. Orlando, FL.

Schnider, K., Elhai, J., and Gray, M. (2007). "Coping Style Use Predicts Posttraumatic Stress and Complicated Grief Symptom Severity Among College Students Reporting a Traumatic Loss." *Journal of Counseling Psychology*, Vol 54(3), Jul, 344–350.

Smith, T. and Renk, K. (2007) "Predictors of Academic-Related Stress in College Students: An Examination of Coping, Social Support, Parenting, and Anxiety." *Journal of Student Affairs Research and Practice*, 44(3).

"Stress. It Is Deadly." (2005). www.holisticonline.com. Retrieved June 8, 2011.

Thoits, P. (2010). "Stress and Health: Major Findings and Policy Implications." *Journal of Health and Social Behavior*, 51(S), S41–S53.

Thoits, P. (2013). "Self-Identity, Stress, and Mental Health." In Avison, W., Aneshensel, C., Schieman, S., and Wheaton, B. (Eds.). *Handbook of the Sociology of Mental Health*. Springer.

CHAPTER SUMMARY

Important parts of this chapter:
- Central nervous system
- Peripheral nervous system
- Parts of the brain that deal with stress
- The role of hormones in stress
- Diseases stress can cause or contribute to
- Effects of stress on relationships

The human body is the most complex machine known to humanity. Its workings are still a source of continual research and wonder. It is known that stress and anxiety can negatively affect the body in various ways, including affecting its chemical/hormonal systems. As a speaker, you should be aware of anxiety and stress and how these feelings can manifest themselves by damaging your health, welfare, and relationships. Also be mindful that stress needs an outlet. The management of these outlets can pay dividends in your career and personal relationships.

There are many ways we can relieve stress. Physical exertion such as walking, running, weight training, and swimming are great stress-relief methods. They not only keep us healthy and toned but also give us an outlet for all that energy buildup that stress brings. We can also look for other ways to relieve stress such as mental exertion, where we focus on mind teasers, reading, building things, and watching television. These activities give our minds something other to focus on besides the stressor or stressors in our lives.

It is important to have a means to expel that built-up energy that stress can cause. If we do not give the body a stress outlet, that energy just stays pent up inside us. Over time, if stress is not managed, its effects can manifest themselves in the form of heart disease, hormonal changes, and accelerated aging. Lastly, it is important that we do not self-medicate with drugs or alcohol or engage in addictive behaviors. This form of dealing with stress can bring about its own body- and mind-damage manifestations, which can do a great deal of damage to the body, mind, and personal relationships.

Remember that your body needs outlets for the energy stress creates. These outlets can be as simple as using hand gestures during your speech or as complex as undertaking a new exercise regimen to deal with the stress from a new job. Stress can have both physical and mental effects. The psychology of stress and how it affects how we think, how we act, and how we react is the topic of chapter 4.

CHAPTER 4

THE PSYCHOLOGY OF NERVOUSNESS

In the readings from Chapter 4, "Fear: Can't Live with It, Can't Live without It," and "Responsiveness to a Mindfulness Manipulation Predicts Affect Regarding an Anger-provoking Situation" you will learn about the psychology of stress and nervousness. This will be particularly useful to you as you try to understand your fears and anxieties and what you can do about them. As you work thorough these readings, think about the things you fear and why you fear them. Do they stem from experiences in your past dealing with your childhood or adolescence, or have they arisen in your adulthood? Do they seem to be of a passing nature, or are they more deep-seated in nature? Do certain situations seem to make these fears manifest themselves?

In this chapter you want to recognize and become mindful of your fears as they relate to anxiety and nervousness related to public speaking. This is important because to overcome your fear or fears, the fear or fears must be specific and not generic. Thus, becoming mindful of specific fears, for example, the fear of your mind going blank in front of the audience during a speech, can help you identify what to do about that specific fear. One way to deal with this fear is to have notes or PowerPoint presentation aids as a memory aid in the advent of a "mind blank".

Use these readings to create in your mind an understanding of your fears and some ways you think you might deal with these fears. The goals here are to both recognize and acknowledge your fears, and to confront and overcome them as they relate to anxiety and nervousness in public speaking. In later chapters you will use this information to help you decide which fear or fears to focus on and overcome as you deal with anxiety and nervousness associated with public speaking. This will help you along as you learn to deal with and overcome public speaking fear and anxiety.

FEAR: CAN'T LIVE WITH IT, CAN'T LIVE WITHOUT IT

by Scott O. Lilienfeld

One of the first clients I treated in my therapy training in clinical psychology in the early 1980s was a 22-year-old college senior psychology major I'll call James. In almost all domains of life, James was successful and self-assured. Yet he had bumped up against a seemingly insurmountable obstacle. To graduate, James needed to pass the required course in laboratory methods that compelled students to conduct a few simple learning demonstrations with rats, of which James had been morbidly afraid since childhood. Working with James, I first came to appreciate just how paralyzing fear can be.

He'd never been bitten by a rat, and had seen a live rat only once, scurrying away from a garbage dump at night. But the mere prospect of interacting with a rat had filled James with such abject terror that he'd postponed the course for several years, hoping beyond hope that he'd somehow find a way of surmounting his fear in the interim. He hadn't. Now he was confronted with an unenviable choice: drop out of college or get over his fear. He selected the latter.

James proved to be the ideal client: motivated, cooperative, and insightful. He understood that his fear was irrational, but was at a complete loss to know what to do about it. So we began by jointly constructing a hierarchy of fear-provoking experiences, starting with situations that James was certain he could handle with minimal anxiety—such as looking at a photograph of a rat in a book—and eventually working our way up to his holding a live pet rat. Yet during our second session, James found that merely viewing a photo of a rat suddenly was too much to handle, as if he were overcome by the looming ultimate step. We went back to the drawing board and decided to begin with his viewing a cartoon drawing of a rat, but even that step proved too anxiety-generating. Finally, we settled on his starting by looking at the word "rat" from a distance, an experience that triggered only mild anxiety. Over the next two months of weekly sessions, we gradually worked our way up our agreed-upon ladder of fear-provoking stimuli, culminating in his handling a real-life rat. James conquered his fear, sailed through the laboratory methods course, and graduated with a B.A.

FEARS FALL INTO CATEGORIES

Fear, it's safe to say, is an emotion most of us would prefer to live without. When fears become extreme, as was the case with James, they manifest themselves as phobias: intense, irrational apprehension of places, objects, or situations. Such fears can assume a seemingly endless variety of forms. Among the more esoteric are coulrophobia (fear of clowns), paraskavedekatriaphobia (fear of Friday the 13th). consecotaleophobia (fear of chopsticks), taphophobia (fear of being buried alive), and arachibutyrophobia (fear of peanut butter sticking to the roof of one's mouth).

Yet this apparent diversity is deceptive, because we can subsume most phobias under a small number of categories. The most recent (fourth) edition of the American Psychiatric Association's *Diagnostic and Statistical Manual of Mental*

Disorders identifies four subtypes of "specific phobia," the most widespread version of pathological fear:

- **Natural-environment phobia,** the fear of heights, water, thunderstorms, and darkness. These are among the stimuli that Martin E. P. Seligman, best-selling author, psychology professor and director of the Positive Psychology Center at University of Pennsylvania, in a 1971 article in the journal *Behavior Therapy*, called "prepared," meaning that we're predisposed evolutionarily to fear them because of the risks they posed to our ancestors. For instance, Phil Rizzuto, Hall of Fame Yankees shortstop and legendary sportscaster, had such an intense phobia of lightning that he would routinely leave the announcer's booth during thunderstorms.

- **Animal phobia**, with dogs, cats, snakes, insects, and spiders receiving top billing. Such phobias usually begin in childhood and commonly dissipate by adolescence, perhaps because most children as they age have repeated uneventful encounters with animals.

- **Situational phobias,** typically the fear of specific situations, like closed-in spaces (claustrophobia), tunnels, elevators, airplanes, and motor vehicles. Situational phobias commonly overlap with a more pervasive condition called **agoraphobia,** a fear of an array of situations in which panic attacks—sudden surges of terror—are likely.

- **Blood/injury/injection phobia,** the fear of blood, injury, medical shots, or deformity. In contrast to other phobias, which are marked by sharp increases in heart rate and blood pressure, blood/injection/injury phobia is marked by sharp decreases in heart rate and blood pressure, explaining why it often produces fainting. Many psychologists suspect that this cardiovascular response is a residue of an evolutionarily adaptive reaction: When we're losing blood, we want our heart and blood vessels to tamp down output to help survival.

Given that most of us don't exactly enjoy pondering our own inevitable demise, we might expect the most common fear to be of death (thanatophobia). Yet population surveys show that fear of public speaking (glossophobia) comes in at number one, while fear of death usually ranks a distant second. When fear of public speaking reaches excessive proportions, it becomes social phobia, also called social anxiety disorder. People with social phobia are petrified of situations in which they could become embarrassed or humiliated; they are terrified of how others may perceive them rather than of discrete stimuli, like dogs or needles. Admittedly, more than 90 percent of us become apprehensive prior to giving a speech in front of a large audience, research indicates, but more than 90 percent of us manage to do it. People with social phobia either cannot do it or force themselves to do it while experiencing intense distress. Social phobia may manifest itself in other fears too, such as fears of performing in public, swimming in public, eating in public, writing in public, or more rarely, using public restrooms. Singers Barbra Streisand and Carly Simon are admitted social phobics, a fact that explains why they rarely tour.

Some of the more common phobias include fear of snakes, clowns, spiders, and enclosed spaces such as tunnels. Do any of these frighten you? Or does something else terrify you?

FEAR SERVES USEFUL PURPOSES

One need not be a fervent proponent of evolutionary psychology to accept a basic proposition: Fear, although unpleasant, serves a crucial adaptive function. It alerts us to potential dangers, like a predator or criminal, readying us for what influential Harvard Medical School physiologist Walter Cannon called the "fight-flight reaction" in his 1929 book, *Bodily Changes in Pain, Fear, Hunger, and Rage.* When we become frightened, our heart speeds up and blood vessels constrict (bearing in mind the exception of blood/injury/injection phobia), allowing more blood to pour into our extremities and preparing us either to fight or flee. In reality, this reaction is better thought of as the fight-flight-freeze reaction, as some species, such as deer or rabbits, become motionless when terrified, probably because many predators rely on movement to detect potential prey.

Facial expressions associated with fear also impart a clear evolutionary story. As clinical psychologist Paul Ekman points out in his important 2007 book. *Emotions Revealed,* across all human cultures fear is characterized by a widening of the eyes, a dilation of the pupils, and a flaring of the nostrils. Each of these telltale signs of fear maximizes our sensory input, helping us to detect potential hazards, like an oncoming car. Moreover, because *Homo sapiens* is a social species, we are exquisitely attuned to signals of fear in others. Research shows that when flashed photographs of others' facial expressions of a few seconds or less, most of us are quicker to pick up fear than other emotions. This finding makes evolutionary sense, because if those around us are scared, they may have detected a threat of which we're unaware.

Psychologically, fear renders us oversensitive to dangers. By doing so, fear often distorts reality. But as the evolutionary principle of "adaptive conservatism" reminds us, better safe than sorry. Indeed, research using computerized images shows that people with phobias overestimate the extent to which feared stimuli, like photographs of spiders, are hurtling toward them. As a German proverb notes, "Fear makes the wolf bigger than he is."

EXTERNAL AND INTERNAL FACTORS CAUSE FEAR

If tear is generally adaptive, why does it sometimes become maladaptive? As clinical psychologist David Barlow, founder/director of the Center for Anxiety and Related Disorders at Boston University, notes in his 2004 book, *Anxiety and its Disorders*, we can conceptualize fear disorders as "false alarms." They reflect the triggering of a fight-flight response in the absence of genuine danger. Virtually all of us would experience a full-blown panic attack while drowning or being chased by a lion, but the threats in such cases would be real and the fight-flight response helpful to our survival. In panic disorder, in contrast, we witness identical patterns of physiological arousal, like racing heart, sweating and hyperventilating, but in situations that are objectively safe, such as an afternoon stroll in a marketplace. So, fear disorders reflect the activation of an otherwise adaptive response that has gone awry for still largely mysterious genetic and environmental reasons.

Although fear surely has deep-seated evolutionary roots, it is just as surely shaped by culture. Some sea hunters in Greenland suffer from "kayak angst," a marked fear of going out in kayaks and an intense desire to return to land, despite the necessity of such travel, for instance, to hunt fish. Kayak angst bears conspicuous similarities to the Western condition of panic disorder with agoraphobia. Some individuals in Asian cultures, especially Japan, experience "taijin kyofusho," which appears to be an Eastern variant of social phobia and is characterized by a fear of offending others, most typically by one's behavior, appearance, or body odor. Interestingly, most Asian cultures are more "collectivist"—concerned with *group harmony*—than are Western cultures, so taijin kyofusho may reflect the manifestation of extreme social anxiety in societies in which upsetting others is a cardinal sin.

Gender plays a role, too. In a groundbreaking 2000 article in *Psychological Review*. University of California, Los Angeles, psychology professor Shelley E. Taylor, director of the school's Social Neuroscience Lab, and her colleagues amassed a substantial body of evidence to show that when frightened, women are more likely than men to display a "tend and befriend" response, as opposed to the better known fight-flight response. That is, when afraid, women more often turn to nurturing and bonding with others, including their children and friends. As even causal viewers of HBO's *Sex and the City* know, women often gravitate toward their close buddies (ideally, at upscale New York City restaurants) when stressed out by work or romance.

PSYCHOPATHS LACK FEAR

The proposition that fear is adaptive leads to a straightforward prediction: People without sufficient fear should be psychologically impaired. In their 1996 book, *Why We Get Sick: The New Science of Darwinian Medicine*, the noted evolutionary theorists Randolph M. Nesse and George C. Williams posited the existence of a yet-to-be-discovered disorder: "hypophobia," or fearlessness. In reality, we needn't look terribly far for such a condition, as psychologists and psychiatrists have recognized it for decades. First described systematically by Hervey M. Cleckley in his trailblazing 1941 book, *The Mask of Sanity*, it's termed psychopathic personality, or psychopathy. Psychopaths, as they're called colloquially, tend to be superficially charming, yet guiltless, callous, egocentric, and dishonest. They're often prone to antisocial and criminal behaviors, like pick-pocketing, shoplifting, fraud, and, in extreme cases, violence. Some psychologists have suggested that bank robber John Dillinger, serial killer Ted Bundy, and convicted swindler Bernard Madoff embody the cardinal features of psychopathy.

If you think a life free of fear is easy, think again. The paucity of fear can be every bit as maladaptive as its surfeit. In a 1957 article in the *Journal of Abnormal and Social Psychology*, University of Minnesota psychophysiological scholar and behavioral geneticist David T. Lykken argued that psychopaths possess a "low fear IQ," or more technically, a high threshold for experiencing fear, allowing them to take physical and social risks that would unnerve the rest of us. In classic research reviewed in his 1995 book, the *Antisocial Personalities*, Lykken discovered that psychopaths don't develop adequate conditioned associations between neutral tones paired repeatedly with electric shock. When presented with the tones alone, psychopaths—in striking contrast to the rest of us—barely respond physiologically. Consequently,

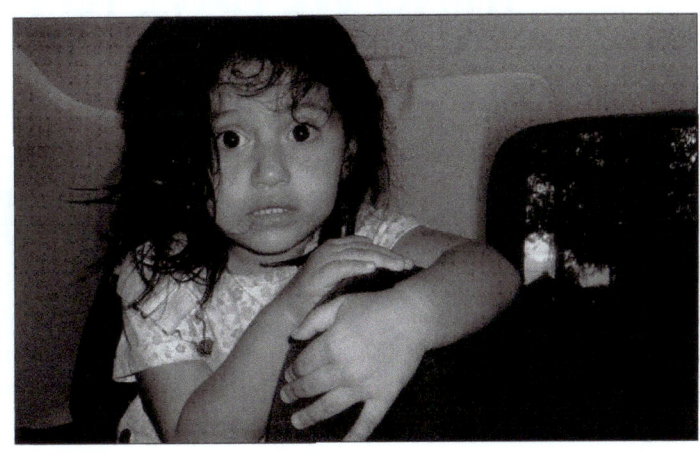

they don't become frightened in anticipation of signals of impending threat. (Interestingly, their response to the shock itself is essentially identical to that of normals.) In a 1966 study, also published in the *Journal of Abnormal and Social Psychology*, influential researcher and academic Robert Hare found that when asked to wait for an electric shock (or, in later research, a joltingly loud noise), psychopaths display markedly lower skin conductance responses—a good index of arousal—than do nonpsychopaths, again suggesting a deficit in fear sensitivity. This fear deficit may render children susceptible to many of the features of psychopathy like lack of guilt and empathy. Fear, after all, is an essential socializing agent for parents and teachers. Without fear, children have little motivation to learn from their mistakes or to predict the negative reactions of powerful others. As the philosopher Nietzsche observed, "Fear is the mother of morality."

Why, then, have psychopaths not been pruned out of the population by natural selection? We don't know. One tantalizing possibility is that psychopaths' fear deficiency, although generally maladaptive, may be adaptive in selected settings. Research by clinical psychologists and university professors Stephen D. Benning, Christopher J, Patrick, and colleagues published in *Psychological Assessment* in 2003 suggests that a key component of psychopathy is fearless dominance, a blend of physical and social boldness. People with high levels of fearless dominance—a subset of whom are psychopaths—may be overrepresented in certain "adaptive niches," like business, politics, entertainment, contact sports, firefighting, and law enforcement, in which their boldness affords them a competitive edge over their timorous peers (although of course the bulk of people in these occupations will never become psychopaths). Still, the scientific support for this hypothesis is preliminary.

WHAT IS, THEN, THE ONLY THING WE HAVE TO FEAR?

All of this brings us to an intriguing conclusion. Much as we'd like to live without fear, most of us need it, at least in moderate doses. Even my early client James knew he had to overcome his fear of rats and was afraid of what would happen if he didn't; without his healthy fear of dropping out of college, James might never have sought treatment. Natural selection may have predisposed the bulk of us to experience intermediate levels of fear, but allowed a few of us with low levels of fear to thrive in certain vocations and avocations—and perhaps capitalize on the fears of the rest of us. Novelist Henry Miller may have gotten it right: "There is nothing strange about fear: No matter in what guise it presents itself it is something with which we are allso familiar that when a man appears who is without it we are at once enslaved by him."

Scott O. Lilienfeld (University of Minnesota), Professor of Psychology at Emory University, is author or co-author of several books, including *50 Great Myths of Popular Psychology: Shattering Widespread Misconceptions about Human Behavior* (with Steven Jay Lynn, John Ruscio, and Barry L. Beyerstein; Wiley-Blackwell, 2010), and more than 200 articles and chapters on psychopathic personality, psychiatric classification and diagnosis, anxiety disorders, evidence-based practice in clinical psychology, and pseudo· science in psychology. Educated at Cornell University (B.A. in Psychology) and University of Minnesota (Ph.D. in Clinical Psychology), he is a fellow of the Association for Psychological Science, editor of *The Scientific Review of Mental Health Practice*, and past president of the Society for a Science of Clinical Psychology. Email him at slilien@emory.edu.

RESPONSIVENESS TO A MINDFULNESS MANIPULATION PREDICTS AFFECT REGARDING AN ANGER-PROVOKING SITUATION

by Catherine N. M. Ortner and Philip David Zelazo

We examined the relation between individual differences in response to a brief mindfulness manipulation and affective reactions to a conflict-provoking situation. Participants recalled a recent personal situation of conflict. They wrote about the event for 10 min and rated their anger and affect on the Positive and Negative Affect Schedule (PANAS) before participating in 1 of 3 10-min manipulations: a mindfulness manipulation, a neutral distraction manipulation, or no manipulation. Participants then completed the Toronto Mindfulness Scale (TMS) before writing about the

Catherine N. M. Ortner and Philip David Zelazo, "Responsiveness to a Mindfulness Manipulation Predicts Affect Regarding an Anger-Provoking Situation," *Canadian Journal of Behavioural Science*, vol. 46, no. 2, pp. 117-124. Copyright © 2014 by Canadian Psychological Association. Reprinted with permission. Provided by ProQuest LLC. All rights reserved.

same event a second time. Finally, participants completed ratings of affect (PANAS) and self-reported anger again. There were no between-groups differences in TMS-Curiosity scores, but TMS–Decentering scores were higher after distraction than after mindfulness or no manipulation. Anger and negative affect significantly decreased from pre- to postmanipulation for all 3 groups. Tests of simple slopes indicated that TMS–Decentering and TMS–Curiosity scores predicted reductions of negative affect and anger in the mindfulness group, suggesting that the mindfulness manipulation was effective for only a subset of individuals, perhaps those higher in dispositional mindfulness.

Keywords: mindfulness, negative affect, distraction, anger

Mindfulness is intended to cultivate continuous attention to ongoing subjective experience together with an attitude of acceptance toward that experience (e.g., Brown & Ryan, 2003; Kabat-Zinn, 1990; Lau et al., 2006). Mindfulness-based practices are increasingly being applied in the treatment of disorders such as depression (Ma & Teasdale, 2004), anxiety (Craigie, Rees, Marsh, & Nathan, 2008), and borderline personality disorder (Linehan, 1993), as well as in the reduction of stress (Carmody & Baer, 2009). There is a growing body of evidence that mindfulness can have positive effects on psychological well-being and mental health, as well as on physical health (see Brown, Ryan & Creswell, 2007, for a review). Researchers have recently turned their attention to examining how mindfulness produces salubrious effects, and some authors (e.g., Stein, Ives-Deliperi, & Thomas, 2008) have proposed that mindfulness is a form of emotion regulation. Others have compared the effects of mindfulness with traditionally studied emotion regulation strategies (Arch & Craske, 2006; Low, Stanton, & Bower, 2008).

Researchers in the field of emotion regulation have typically examined strategies, such as suppression and reappraisal, that are used to downregulate or diminish emotions (e.g., Gross, 1998, 2001). For example, reappraisal is a cognitive strategy that involves changing the way one thinks about an emotional stimulus in order to diminish its impact, while suppression involves hiding any outward displays of emotion. In contrast, mindfulness involves accepting whatever stimuli arise (including emotional experiences) without trying to change them (Chambers, Gullone, & Allen, 2009; Kabat-Zinn, 1990). In an extensive review of the relation between mindfulness and emotion regulation, Chambers et al. suggested that mindfulness reduces suppression and avoidance, while changing the nature of the relationship to emotions. Mindfulness is intended to promote a more flexible, open approach (Hayes & Wilson, 2003) and foster metacognitive awareness, or a decentred perspective, in which subjective experiences are viewed as transient events rather than as permanent aspects of the self (Teasdale, 1999; Teasdale, Segal, & Williams, 1995). This may reduce rumination (Teasdale et al., 1995) and knee-jerk reactions to emotionally evocative stimuli while facilitating choice over to which stimuli one should attend (Chambers et al., 2009).

There are a number of studies providing correlational evidence of a relation between mindfulness and emotion regulation using questionnaire measures (e.g., Lykins & Baer, 2009; Roemer et al., 2009). In addition, there is a growing experimental literature on changes in mindfulness and emotion as a result of mindfulness meditation training in both clinical and nonclinical populations (e.g., Kumar, Feldman, & Hayes, 2008; Ortner, Kilner, & Zelazo, 2007). These studies suggest that mindfulness training reduces negative affect, and that the effects can be seen after relatively brief (7 to 24 weeks) training interventions.

There are just a handful of experimental studies that have attempted to induce mindfulness or facets of mindfulness (e.g., acceptance) in the labouratory and compared it with other emotion regulation strategies. For example, Arch and Craske (2006) found that participants who view neutral, positive, and aversive picture slides before and after a 15-min focused breathing induction were more willing than control participants to view optional negative slides. They also reported reduced negative affect to neutral, but not negative, slides. In another study, participants who completed a mindfulness manipulation reported less negative affect after an affectively mixed film clip and more positive affect after a positive film clip, in comparison with a control group (Erisman & Roemer, 2010). However, there were no differences between the two groups on negative affect or emotion regulation difficulties after viewing a distressing film clip. Finally, participants who wrote about a stressful experience in an accepting way showed no differences in heart rate reactivity and recovery in comparison with a control group (Low et al., 2008). Thus, research to date suggests that laboratory manipulations designed to induce the state of mindfulness in participants (without providing more extensive training in mindfulness practices) have only limited effectiveness in reducing negative affect. One possibility is that there are individual differences in responsiveness to the mindfulness manipulation, with only a subset of participants responding favourably to the manipulation. To date, while some studies have explored the relation between trait mindfulness and dispositional measures of affect (e.g., Jimenez, Niles, & Park, 2010; Roemer et al., 2009), there has been little exploration of the relation between dispositional mindfulness and the response to emotional induction in the labouratory. One exception is the finding that trait or dispositional mindfulness correlates with neural changes in brain regions, reflecting reduced affective responsiveness when labelling affect in negative emotional stimuli (Creswell, Way, Eisenberger, & Lieberman, 2007). Other recent research has found that trait mindfulness predicts the response of clinically anxious and nonanxious participants to laboratory stressors designed to induce anxiety (Arch & Craske, 2010). These findings suggest that individual differences in mindfulness can predict responses to emotionally provocative stimuli in the labouratory.

A further limitation of some of the described studies is that the emotional stimuli—unpleasant pictures from the International Affective Picture System (IAPS; Lang, Bradley, & Cuthbert, 2008) or emotionally provocative film clips—were not necessarily personally relevant to the participants. Yet, people practising mindfulness techniques, whether in clinical settings or in their own practice, are often struggling with stressors in their daily lives that are indeed personally relevant. Thus, it may be valuable to examine how mindfulness can be used to regulate emotions regarding personally salient events (cf. Low et al., 2008).

In the current study, we wished to ascertain whether a mindfulness manipulation involving awareness and acceptance would help reduce negative affect and anger in response to a recent personal situation of conflict. In this context, the mindfulness manipulation included instructions to focus one's awareness on one's breathing and to respond to any loss of focus with an attitude of acceptance. We explored whether individual differences in response to the manipulation would predict changes in affect. Participants recalled a recent event of conflict that involved someone close to them (e.g., close friend, colleague, family member, or partner) and that they were feeling angry or upset about. Participants wrote about the event, completed a brief mindfulness manipulation, and then wrote about the event again. Two control conditions consisted of participants either completing a neutral distraction or experiencing no manipulation. We expected that participants would report reduced feelings of anger and negative affect after the mindfulness manipulation. In addition, we expected that higher mindfulness scores in the mindfulness manipulation condition would be associated with reduced feelings of anger and negative affect. We also predicted that writing samples in the mindfulness condition would contain fewer expressions of negative emotion and anger and more positive emotion words. Research by Weintraub (1989) has indicated that angry speech contains an increased use of negations (such as "not" and "never"), with a reduction in the use of qualifiers. If, as suggested by some authors (e.g., Hayes et al., 2003; Teasdale, 1999), mindfulness promotes flexibility and a decentered perspective, and results in reduced feelings of anger and negative affect, it should result in fewer negations and an increase in words indicating a more tentative approach (such as "maybe" and "perhaps").

METHOD

PARTICIPANTS

Fifty-two undergraduate students from the introductory psychology participant pool of a large urban university were randomly assigned to one of three conditions: distraction ($n = 19$), mindfulness ($n = 18$), or no manipulation ($n = 15$).

MEASURES

Positive and Negative Affect Schedule (PANAS; Watson, Clark, & Tellegen, 1988). The PANAS consists of 20 affective descriptors, 10 positive and 10 negative (e.g., "enthusiastic," "jittery"). For each descriptor, respondents rated on a 5-point scale from 1 (*very slightly or not at all*) to 5 (*extremely*) the extent to which they had experienced the described affective state during the past few weeks. Mean scores on the PANAS can range from 1 to 5 for each scale, with 5 indicating high levels of either positive or negative affect. In previous research, alpha reliabilities were .86 and .87 for positive affect and negative affect scales, respectively, and the expected high positive correlations with measures of distress and psychopathology, such as the Beck Depression Inventory and the Hopkins Symptom Checklist, have also been found. We computed mean scores for positive and negative affect, pre- and postmanipulation. For the current data, alpha reliabilities were as follows: positive affect scale, premanipulation: .88, 95% confidence interval (CI) [.83, .92], postmanipulation: .88, 95% CI [.82, .92]; negative affect scale, premanipulation: .87, 95% CI [.81, .92], postmanipulation: .75, 95% CI [.63, .84].

Toronto Mindfulness Scale (TMS; Lau et al., 2006). The TMS is a 13-item scale that assesses Curiosity (e.g., "I was curious about what I might learn about myself by taking notice of how I react to certain thoughts, feelings or sensations"; "I was curious about my reactions to things") and Decentering (e.g., "I experienced my thoughts more as events in my mind than as a necessarily accurate reflection of the way things 'really' are"; "I approached each experience by trying to accept it, no matter whether it was pleasant or unpleasant"). In selecting a measure of mindfulness, we required a scale that would enable the assessment of group differences in state mindfulness after exposure to the manipulation. At the time of conducting the study, the TMS was the only measure in the literature that met these requirements. Participants normally complete the TMS after being instructed, "For the next 15 minutes, please pay attention to your breathing and anything that might arise during your experience," or after practising a mindfulness meditation technique. Mean scores on the TMS range from 0 to 4, with higher scores reflecting greater mindfulness. Alpha reliability values for the TMS are .88 for the Curiosity factor and .84 for the Decentering factor, and the factors have been shown to correlate significantly with related measures, such as Absorption, Reflective Self-Awareness, and Psychological Mindedness (Lau et al., 2006). In the current study, participants completed the TMS after the 10-min manipulation (distraction, mindfulness, or no manipulation). We calculated mean scores for Decentering and Curiosity. No baseline TMS was administered to reduce the likelihood that demand characteristics would influence responding during the postmanipulation administration of the TMS. For the current data, alpha reliability was as follows: .76, 95% CI [.65, .85] for the overall TMS score; .85, 95% CI [.78, .91] for Curiosity; and .52, 95% CI [.29, .70] for Decentering.

Anger rating. Participants rated how angry they felt about the situation (1 = *not at all angry*, 5 = *extremely angry*).

Linguistic analysis. We analysed participants' written statements using the Linguistic Inquiry and Word Count (LIWC; Pennebaker, Chung, Ireland, Gonzales, & Booth, 2007). The LIWC is text analysis software that provides counts of the number of words and word stems that fall into approximately 80 linguistic categories, based on a dictionary of almost 4500 words and word stems, developed by Pennebaker et al. (2007). For the current study, the word categories of interest were the number of positive (e.g., love, nice) and negative emotion words (e.g., hurt, nasty), anger words (e.g., hate, kill), negations (e.g., not, never), and tentative words (e.g., maybe, perhaps). Previous work has assessed the validity of the LIWC dictionary categories, with correlations between LIWC counts and judge ratings of .41 and .31 for positive and negative emotion words, respectively, and a correlation of .22 for anger words (correlations not available for negations and tentative words; Pennebaker et al.). Pennebaker et al. also found Cronbach's alpha reliability values (for binary and uncorrected methods respectively) as follows: positive emotion words, .97/.40; negative emotion words, .97/.61; anger words, .92/.55; negations, .80/.28; and tentative words, .87/.13.

PROCEDURE

Participants filled out an informed consent form upon entering the laboratory. Participants then completed the tasks independently in a small, sound-proofed testing room where they sat at a desk with a computer. Participants received a booklet containing instructions and the paper-and-pencil measures. They heard prerecorded instructions for the manipulations via the computer speakers, which they were directed to initiate by pressing a key on the computer keyboard when they reached the appropriate place in the participant booklet.

Participants received the following instructions to write about a situation of conflict. The instructions were adapted from those commonly used in writing studies (e.g., Rude, Gortner, & Pennebaker, 2004). Other studies have found that recall of a recent situation of conflict can be used to elicit affect, which can be modified by different perspective-taking strategies (Kross, Ayduk, & Mischel, 2005). The instructions were as follows:

> What I would like you to do is to write about a recent situation of conflict involving someone close to you (this could be a close friend, colleague, family member, or partner) that has angered you in some way. In your writing, I want you to really let go and explore your very deepest emotions and thoughts about this situation. Please write continuously for the entire time. If you run out of things to say, just repeat what you have already written. In your writing, don't worry about grammar, spelling, or sentence structure. Just write legibly. You will be told when to stop writing.

Despite the instruction for participants to "repeat what [they had] already written," examination of participants' written statements indicated that there was no evidence of redundancy in any of the statements.

After 10 min, participants stopped writing. They then completed the situation rating scales and the PANAS before hearing one of three sets of instructions, according to their manipulation condition. The mindfulness and distraction manipulation instructions were designed to be similar in length (282 words and 319 words, respectively) and were read over the course of the first 3 min and 45 s of the 10-min manipulation. In the mindfulness condition, participants heard instructions based on mindfulness practice instructions given by Segal, Williams, and Teasdale (2002). Participants were directed to attend to their breathing, maintaining their attention in the present moment, noticing and accepting when their attention wandered to thoughts or feelings, and bringing their attention back to their breathing. In the distraction condition, participants followed a guided imagery exercise, imagining the house or apartment where they live in great detail, paying attention to what they see, hear, and touch. In the no-manipulation condition, participants received instructions to sit quietly and wait for a short time. After each minute, a number appeared on the computer monitor in front of them, indicating how many minutes were left. Participants then completed the TMS before writing about the situation of conflict, and completing the PANAS and situation rating scales a second time.

RESULTS

TORONTO MINDFULNESS SCALE (TMS)

To examine the effects of the manipulation on self-reported mindfulness, we conducted two one-way between-subjects analyses of variance (ANOVAs) with manipulation (mindfulness, distraction, and no manipulation) as the independent variable and TMS Curiosity and Decentering scores as the dependent variables. There was a main effect of manipulation on Decentering scores, $F(2, 49) = 7.71$, $p < .005$, partial $\eta^2 = .24$, but no main effect of manipulation on Curiosity scores, $F(2, 49) = .29$, ns, partial $\eta^2 = .01$ (see Table 4.1). Tukey's Honestly Significant Difference (HSD) indicated that Decentering scores were higher in the distraction condition than in the mindfulness condition ($p < .005$) and in the distraction condition than in the no manipulation condition ($p < .01$).

SELF-REPORT

Prior to the manipulation, there were no significant differences on any of the self-report measures: anger: $F(2, 49) = .21$, ns, partial $\eta^2 = .01$; negative affect: $F(2, 49) = .67$, ns, partial $\eta^2 = .03$; positive affect: $F(2, 49) = .43$, ns, partial $\eta^2 = .02$ (see Table 4.1). We conducted mixed ANOVAs to examine changes from pre- to postmanipulation, with testing time (pre- vs. postmanipulation) and type of manipulation (mindfulness, distraction, and no manipulation) as the independent variables. Participants reported significantly lower negative affect on the PANAS postmanipulation in comparison with premanipulation, $F(1, 48) = 15.42$, $p < .001$, partial $\eta^2 = .24$, and less anger, $F(1, 48) = 22.44$, $p < .001$, partial $\eta^2 = .32$. There was no significant change in PANAS positive affect scores, $F(1, 48) = .041$, ns, partial $\eta^2 = .00$. There was no significant effect of manipulation, nor were there any significant interactions between manipulation type and testing time on any of the self-report measures.

LINGUISTIC ANALYSES

Prior to the manipulation, there were no significant differences among groups on any of the examined LIWC categories. Means and standard deviations for the

Table 4.1 Mean Scores and Standard Deviations for Mindfulness (Curiosity and Decentering) and Affect (Positive and Negative), Before and After Manipulation

			CONDITION			
	MINDFULNESS (**N** = 18)		DISTRACTION (**N** = 19)		NO MANIPULATION (**N** = 15)	
SCALE	PRE	POST	PRE	POST	PRE	POST
TMS-Curiosity						
M	—	2.19	—	1.97	—	2.03
SD	—	0.98	—	1.00	—	0.64
TMS-Decentering						
M	—	1.90	—	2.47	—	1.90
SD	—	0.55	—	0.51	—	0.44
Anger						
M	3.44	2.61	3.32	2.56	3.20	2.47
SD	1.20	1.09	1.20	1.29	0.76	0.92
PANAS-Negative						
M	2.16	1.68	2.26	1.66	1.93	1.71
SD	0.87	0.50	0.82	0.61	0.76	0.63
PANAS-Positive						
M	2.16	2.27	2.42	2.30	2.31	2.39
SD	0.89	0.74	0.82	0.86	0.79	0.88

Note. TMS = Toronto Mindfulness Scale; PANAS = Positive and Negative Affect Schedule.

LIWC analyses are presented in Table 4.2. Mean values for all categories examined fell within 1 standard deviation of the means reported by Pennebaker et al. (2007), which were based on 2800 randomly selected texts in a variety of genres, including emotional and control writing, science articles, blogs, novels, and talking. We conducted mixed ANOVA analyses to examine changes in word use in the written essays from pre- to postmanipulation, with testing time (pre- vs. postmanipulation) and type of manipulation (mindfulness, distract, and no manipulation) as the independent variables. There was a significant increase in positive emotion words from pre- to postmanipulation, $F(1, 48) = 6.51$, $p < .01$, partial $\eta^2 = .12$, and an increase

Table 4.2 Mean Scores and Standard Deviations for Word Use, Before and After Manipulation

	CONDITION					
	MINDFULNESS (N = 18)		DISTRACTION (N = 19)		NO MANIPULATION (N = 15)	
MANIPULATION	PRE	POST	PRE	POST	PRE	POST
Positive emotion						
M	2.86	3.45	2.59	3.77	3.29	3.19
SD	1.55	1.41	0.90	1.57	1.67	1.33
Negative emotion						
M	2.77	3.42	3.60	3.79	3.19	3.40
SD	1.56	1.52	1.91	2.12	1.69	1.95
Anger words						
M	1.17	1.19	1.47	1.77	1.47	1.44
SD	1.00	0.77	1.08	1.54	0.91	1.30
Tentative words						
M	2.62	3.06	2.31	2.61	2.34	2.57
SD	1.40	1.40	1.12	0.94	1.60	1.19
Negations						
M	1.14	1.16	0.80	1.27	1.18	1.54
SD	0.75	0.84	0.48	0.90	1.18	0.78

in the number of negations, $F(1, 48) = 4.41$, $p < .05$, partial $\eta^2 = .08$. However, there was no change in negative emotion words, $F(1, 48) = 2.35$, ns, partial $\eta^2 = .05$; anger words, $F(1, 48) = .519$, ns, partial $\eta^2 = .01$; or tentative words, $F(1, 48) = 2.14$, ns, partial $\eta^2 = .04$ (see Table 4.2). There was no significant effect of manipulation on positive or negative emotion words, or anger words, $F(2, 48) = .02$, ns, partial $\eta^2 = .00$; $F(2, 48) = .65$, ns, partial $\eta^2 = .03$; and $F(2, 48) = .87$, ns, partial $\eta^2 = .04$, respectively. There was also no effect of manipulation on tentative words and negations, $F(2, 48) = .81$, ns, partial $\eta^2 = .03$; $F(2, 48) = .95$, ns, partial $\eta^2 = .04$, respectively. There was no significant interaction between testing time and type of manipulation for any of the linguistic analyses.

SIMPLE SLOPES ANALYSES

In order to test the prediction that differences in responses to the mindfulness manipulation may predict changes in negative affect and anger, we conducted tests of the simple slopes (Aiken & West, 1991), for each manipulation condition separately, for the regression of Curiosity and Decentering scores on changes in negative affect and anger. Difference scores (pre and post) were computed as an index of change, with higher scores reflecting a greater reduction in negative affect or anger. Six regressions were conducted, using dummy coding to test the simple slopes for each manipulation condition separately, with condition, Curiosity, and the interaction between condition and Curiosity as the predictor variables. Curiosity scores predicted reductions in negative affect and anger for the mindful condition only, $\beta = .613$, $t(50) = 2.99$, $p < .005$, and $\beta = .626$, $t(50) = 3.17$, $p < .005$, with higher Curiosity scores associated with greater reductions in negative affect and anger. Curiosity was also associated with reductions in anger in the distraction condition, $\beta = .395$, $t(50) = 2.07$, $p < .05$. There was no relation between Curiosity and changes in negative affect and anger in the no manipulation condition. For Decentering, six regressions were conducted, using dummy coding to test the simple slopes for each manipulation condition separately, with condition, Decentering, and the interaction between condition and Decentering as the predictor variables. Decentering scores predicted reductions in negative affect and anger in the mindfulness condition only, $\beta = .518$, $t(50) = 2.12$, $p < .05$, and $\beta = .500$, $t(50) = 2.04$, $p < .05$, respectively, with higher Decentering scores associated with greater reductions in negative affect and anger from pre- to postmanipulation. There was no relation between Decentering and changes in negative affect and anger in the distraction and no manipulation conditions.

DISCUSSION

The goal of the current study was to examine the effects of a brief mindfulness manipulation on people's self-reported affect and the language of their written statements about a situation of personal conflict. In addition, we wished to explore how individual differences in responses to the mindfulness manipulation predicted changes in self-reported affect. Participants wrote about a situation of personal conflict before and after completing either a mindfulness manipulation, a distraction manipulation, or no manipulation. Results indicate changes in affect and language from pre- to postmanipulation in all three conditions. Self-reported anger and negative affect decreased from pre- to postmanipulation, regardless of the type of manipulation. However, higher Curiosity and Decentering scores were associated with reduced self-reported ratings of anger and negative affect in the mindfulness group, with only Curiosity predicting reductions in anger in the distraction group, and no association between mindfulness (Curiosity or Decentering scores) and affect or anger in the no manipulation group. These findings help shed some light on the specific benefits of mindfulness interventions, and they also add to the burgeoning literature on the effects of writing on emotional well-being.

Although there were no differences in self-reported affect as a result of the different manipulations, higher-state Decentering and Curiosity scores in the mindfulness condition predicted greater self-reported reductions in anger and negative affect. This finding suggests that the mindfulness manipulation may only be effective for a subset of individuals. One possibility is that some individuals attained greater affective benefits because they were more easily able to enter a mindful state. This may also be related to trait mindfulness, which was not measured in the current study. These findings accord with research by Creswell et al. (2007), showing that higher dispositional mindfulness is associated with greater reductions in amygdala activity when labelling affect in negatively valenced stimuli. We also noted an unexpected relation between reductions in anger and Curiosity in the distraction condition, suggesting that distraction may have conferred benefits for some individuals. However, the observation that the relation between mindfulness and affective change was primarily confined to the mindfulness condition and that the size of that change (as indicated by the higher values for the standardized regression coefficients) was larger in the mindfulness condition, suggests that high dispositional mindfulness in combination with a mindfulness manipulation may be particularly effective in reducing affective responsiveness. Unfortunately, because we did not measure dispositional mindfulness using the TMS in its original form, we were unable to assess whether this correlation would hold in the absence of a mindfulness manipulation. This issue should be addressed in future research.

Contrary to our initial predictions, affective language use after the manipulation did not change differentially in the mindfulness condition. To our knowledge, there have been no other studies examining changes in language use after a brief mindfulness manipulation. Future studies could explore whether longer mindfulness interventions give rise to changes in affective language use.

In summary, the current findings provide experimental evidence of the effect of a mindfulness manipulation on affect. Importantly, the findings suggest that in a sample of individuals who likely have little prior experience with mindfulness, the affective benefits of such a brief (10 min) manipulation may be limited to a subset of individuals who are more responsive to the manipulation—perhaps those who are higher in dispositional mindfulness, and who are more easily able to enter a mindful state and thus experience benefits from the manipulation. Future work should explore the relation between dispositional mindfulness and response to both brief mindfulness manipulations and longer interventions.

The finding that anger and negative affect decreased for all conditions in our study (including the control condition in which participants simply waited for 10 min before completing their second writing task) suggests that simply writing about a situation of personal conflict can reduce anger and negative affect for the writer. This is consistent with an abundance of studies on the benefits of expressive writing for physical and emotional wellbeing in healthy adults as well as those dealing with physical ailments and psychopathology (see Esterling, L'Abate, Murray, & Pennebaker, 1999, and Frattaroli, 2006, for reviews). However, it is important to note that because the main focus of our study was not on the beneficial effects of writing, we did not include an appropriate control condition to explore such changes; it may be that after recalling a situation of conflict, negative affect would have diminished with time regardless of whether or not the participant engaged in the writing task. In addition, it was noted that the scale score reliability coefficients for the negative affect scale of the PANAS were lower postmanipulation than premanipulation. One possibility is that the manipulations prompted a differentiation amongst the various descriptors of negative affect on the PANAS, resulting in lower scale score reliability.

There are several drawbacks to the current study. We found that while distraction resulted in higher Decentering scores, we did not show higher Curiosity and Decentering scores in the mindfulness manipulation condition, suggesting that overall, the mindfulness manipulation may not have induced a mindful state effectively, at least as measured by the TMS. This may be due to the fact that participants were not selected because of any particular prior experience in mindfulness practice, and it is likely that many participants did not have extensive prior experience with the practice of mindfulness. As a result, it may have been difficult for some participants to enter a mindful state, and any changes in mindfulness in this group may have been too small to measure. Indeed, Lau et al. (2006) found that individuals with a longer history of mindfulness meditation practice, as well as those who participated in an 8-week mindfulness-based stress reduction program, scored higher on the TMS than did those with no experience in mindfulness.

In considering why distraction resulted in higher Decentering scores, examination of our distraction instructions indicates that there may be some overlap with the mindfulness instructions, in that participants were required to focus their attention on a particular object. For mindfulness, this object was their breathing; for distraction, this object was the details of the place in which they lived. In a sample of individuals relatively inexperienced with mindfulness, it may be that the focusing of attention on the more vivid details of one's place of residence is easier than the focusing of attention on the breathing. Previous work has also found that awareness of one's own surroundings is positively correlated with decentering (Lau et al., 2006), and distraction may have promoted such awareness and increased Decentering scores. However, the lack of relation between decentering and affect in the distraction group, contrasted with positive associations between reductions in negative affect and decentering in the mindfulness group, suggests that the decentering in the distraction condition may have been qualitatively different from the decentering in the mindfulness condition. A key difference between the mindfulness and distraction conditions was that the mindfulness manipulation included the direction to notice when attention wandered away from the breath, with an emphasis on acceptance and nonjudgment. In contrast, the distraction condition did not include any instructions relating to awareness of the contents of consciousness, or to acceptance and nonjudgment. Rather, it simply emphasised attention to the various external stimuli as the person took the "mental tour" of his or her home.

Another limitation is that the 10-min mindfulness exercise used in the current study was different from the instructions given by Lau et al. in their administration of the TMS. As a result, participants may have entered a different state from what the TMS was designed to measure. The lack of a manipulation check also leaves us uncertain as to the extent to which participants followed the mindfulness or distraction instructions. In addition, we did not assess baseline dispositional mindfulness because of concerns about demand characteristics influencing responses on the postmanipulation TMS. Nor did we ask participants whether they had prior experience with mindfulness. Therefore, we were unable to assess whether there were any preexisting differences among groups that could have accounted for our findings of reduced negative affect in the mindfulness condition. However, it was expected that random assignment of participants to groups would have reduced the likelihood of there being preexisting between-groups differences. Further research is required to rule out the possibility that preexisting group differences accounted for the relation between reduced negative affect and TMS scores in the mindfulness condition.

There are currently multiple measures available to assess mindfulness. We used the TMS, which comprises two factors, but researchers do not agree on whether mindfulness comprises a single factor (e.g., Walach, Buchheld, Buttenmüller, Kleinknecht, & Schmidt, 2006) or multiple factors (e.g., Baer, Smith, & Allen, 2004), nor on what those multiple factors are. In addition, it should be noted that the reliability coefficient for the Decentering subscale of the TMS was low (.52). Researchers have noted that some of the items on the various measures of mindfulness may be confounding facets of the construct of mindfulness with the outcomes of mindfulness practice (Baer, Smith, Hopkins, Krietemeyer, & Toney, 2006). It is uncertain whether our results would be replicated given a different measure of mindfulness.

Despite these limitations, the finding of a significant association between both Decentering and Curiosity TMS scores and greater decreases in negative affect and anger, which was unique to the mindfulness condition, suggests that some individuals may have been more responsive to the mindfulness manipulation. Nonetheless, the current study does indicate that inducing mindfulness in the laboratory in participants who do not have extensive prior mindfulness meditation experience can be challenging. There is other evidence in the literature to support this notion. For example, Arch and Craske (2006) used a focused breathing instruction, similar to ours, on the basis of the work of Kabat-Zinn (1990) and Segal et al. (2002). While they did not assess mindfulness after the manipulation, they did conduct a manipulation check whereby participants rated on a scale of 1 (*very true*) to 7 (*very untrue*) to what extent they had followed the taped induction instructions. Across conditions, participants gave a mean rating of 5.63, indicating that they believed the statement to be a "little untrue." As noted by Arch and Craske, training in mindfulness and greater compliance with the focused breathing instructions may yield larger effects.

A final drawback to the present study is the small sample size. This may have limited our ability to detect significant interaction effects, in particular when combined with the difficulties inherent in attempting to induce mindfulness in participants who may not be familiar with the technique.

In summary, the current study provides a basis for continuing to explore how mindfulness produces positive consequences for wellbeing, in particular through its effects on the processing of personally relevant emotional stimuli. Future research in this area should examine the relation between trait mindfulness and the ease with which participants are able to enter a mindful state, as well as their respective influence on affective responses. It will also be important to compare the effectiveness of different interventions in individuals who have had training in a variety of emotion regulation strategies as well as mindfulness.

REFERENCES

Aiken, L. S., & West, S. G. (1991). *Multiple regression: Testing and interpreting interactions.* Newbury Park, CA: Sage.

Arch, J. J., & Craske, M. G. (2006). Mechanisms of mindfulness: Emotion regulation following a focused breathing induction. *Behaviour Research and Therapy, 44.* 1849–1858. doi:10.10l6/j.brat.2005.12.007.

Arch, J. J., & Craske, M. G. (2010). Laboratory stressors in clinically anxious and non-anxious individuals: The moderating role of mindfulness. *Behaviour Research and Therapy, 48,* 495–505. doi:10.1016/j.brat.2010.02.005.

Baer, R. A., Smith, G. T., & Allen, K. B. (2004). Assessment of mindfulness by self-report: The Kentucky Inventory of Mindfulness Skills. *Assessment, 11*. 191-206. doi:10.1177/1073191104268029.

Baer, R. A., Smith, G. T., Hopkins, J., Krietemeyer, J., & Toney, L. (2006). Using self-report assessment methods to explore facets of mindfulness. *Assessment. 13*, 27-45. doi:10.1177/1073191105283504.

Brown, K. W., & Ryan, R. M. (2003). The benefits of being present: Mindfulness and its role in psychological well-being. *Journal of Personality and Social Psychology, 84*, 822-848. doi:10.l037/0022-3514.84.4.822.

Brown, K. W., Ryan, R. M., & Creswell, J. D. (2007). Mindfulness: Theoretical foundations and evidence for its salutary effects. *Psychological Inquiry. 18*, 211-237. doi:10.1080/10478400701598298.

Carmody, J., & Baer, R. A. (2009). How long does a mindfulness-based stress reduction program need to be? A review of class contact hours and effect sizes for psychological distress. *Journal of Clinical Psychology, 65*. 627-638. doi:10.1002/jclp.20555.

Carmody, J., Baer, R. A., Lykins, E. L. B., & Olendzki, N. (2009). An empirical study of the mechanisms of mindfulness in a mindfulness-based stress reduction program. *Journal of Clinical Psychology, 65*, 613-626. doi:10.1002/jclp.20579.

Chambers, R., Gullone, E., & Allen, N. B. (2009). Mindful emotion regulation: An integrative review. *Clinical Psychology Review, 29*, 560-572. doi:10.1016/j.cpr.2009.06.005.

Craigie, M. A., Rees, C. S., Marsh, A., & Nathan, P. (2008). Mindfulness-based cognitive therapy for generalized anxiety disorder: A preliminary evaluation. *Behavioural and Cognitive Psychotherapy, 36*, 553-568. doi:10.1017/S135246580800458X.

Creswell, J. D., Way, B. M., Eisenberger, N. I., & Lieberman, M. D. (2007). Neural correlates of dispositional mindfulness during affect labeling. *Psychosomatic Medicine, 69*, 560-565. doi:10.1097/PSY.0b013e3180f6171f.

Erisman, S. M., & Roemer, L. (2010). A preliminary investigation of the effects of experimentally induced mindfulness on emotional responding to film clips. *Emotion, 10*, 72-82. doi:10.1037/a0017162.

Esterling, B. A., L'Abate, L., Murray, E. J., & Pennebaker, J. W. (1999). Empirical foundations for writing in prevention and psychotherapy: Mental and physical health outcomes. *Clinical Psychology Review, 19*, 79-96. doi:10.1016/S0272-7358(98)00015-4.

Frattaroli, J. (2006). Experimental disclosure and its moderators: A metaanalysis. *Psychological Bulletin, 132*, 823-865. doi:10.1037/0033-2909.132.6.823.

Gross, J. J. (1998). The emerging field of emotion regulation: An integrative review. *Review of General Psychology, 2*, 271-299. doi:10.1037/ 1089-2680.2.3.271.

Gross, J. J. (2001). Emotion regulation in adulthood: Timing is everything. *Current Directions in Psychological Science, 10*, 214-219. doi:10.1111/1467-8721.00152.

Hayes, S. C., & Wilson, K. G. (2003). Mindfulness: Method and process. *Clinical Psychology: Science and Practice, 10*, 161-165. doi:10.1093/clipsy.bpg018.

Jimenez, S. S., Niles, B. L., & Park, C. L. (2010). A mindfulness model of affect regulation and depressive symptoms: Positive emotions, mood regulation expectancies, and self-acceptance as regulatory mechanisms. *Personality and Individual Differences, 49*, 645-650. doi:10.1016/j.paid.2010.05.041.

Kabat-Zinn, J. (1990). *Full catastrophe living.* New York, NY: Dell.

Kross, E., Ayduk, O., & Mischel, W. (2005). When asking 'Why' does not hurt: Distinguishing rumination from reflective processing of negative emotions. *Psychological Science, 16*, 709-715. doi:10.1111/j.1467-9280.2005.01600.x.

Kumar, S., Feldman, G., & Hayes, A. (2008). Changes in mindfulness and emotion regulation in an exposure-based cognitive therapy for depression. *Cognitive Therapy and Research, 32*, 734-744. doi:10.1007/si 0608-008-9190-1.

Lang, E. J., Bradley, M. M., & Cuthbert, B. N. (2008). *International affective picture system (IAPS): Affective ratings of pictures and instruction manual (Tech. Rep. A-8).* Gainesville, FL: University of Florida.

Lau, M. A., Bishop, S. R., Segal, Z. V., Buis, T., Anderson, N. D., Carlson, L., ... Devins, G. (2006). The Toronto Mindfulness Scale: Development and validation. *Journal of Clinical Psychology, 62,* 1445–1467. doi:10.1002/jclp.20326.

Linehan, M. M. (1993). *Cognitive-behavioral treatment of borderline personality disorder.* New York, NY: Guilford Press.

Low, C. A., Stanton, A. L., & Bower, J. E. (2008). Effects of acceptance-oriented versus evaluative emotional processing on heart rate recovery and habituation. *Emotion. 8.* 419–424. doi:10.1037/1528-3542.8.3.419.

Lykins, E. L. B., & Baer, R. A. (2009). Psychological functioning in a sample of long-term practitioners of mindfulness meditation. *Journal of Cognitive Psychotherapy. 23,* 226–241. doi:10.1891/0889-8391.23.3.226.

Ma, S. H., & Teasdale, J. D. (2004). Mindfulness-based cognitive therapy for depression: Replication and exploration of differential relapse prevention effects. *Journal of Consulting and Clinical Psychology, 72,* 31–40. doi:10.1037/0022-006X.72.1.31.

Ortner, C. N. M., Kilner, S. J., & Zelazo, P. D. (2007). Mindfulness meditation and reduced emotional interference on a cognitive task. *Motivation and Emotion, 31,* 271–283. doi:10.1007/s11031-007-9076-7.

Pennebaker, J. W., Chung, C. K., Ireland, M., Gonzales, A., & Booth, R. J. (2007). *The development and psychometric properties of LIWC2007.* Austin, TX: LIWC.net.

Roemer, L., Lee, J. K., Salters-Pedneault, K., Erisman, S. M., Orsillo, S. M., & Mennin, D. S. (2009). Mindfulness and emotion regulation difficulties in generalized anxiety disorder: Preliminary evidence for independent and overlapping contributions. *Behavior Therapy, 40,* 142–154. doi:10.1016/j.beth.2008.04.001.

Rude, S., Gortner, E., & Pennebaker, J. (2004). Language use of depressed and depression-vulnerable college students. *Cognition and Emotion, 18,* 1121–1133. doi:10.1080/02699930441000030.

Segal, Z. V., Williams, J. M., & Teasdale, J. D. (2002). *Mindfulness-based cognitive therapy for depression: A new approach to preventing relapse.* New York, NY: Guilford Press.

Stein, D. J., Ives-Deliperi, V., & Thomas, K. G. F. (2008). Psychobiology of mindfulness. *CNS Spectrums, 13,* 752–756.

Teasdale, J. D. (1999). Emotional processing, three modes of mind and the prevention of relapse in depression. *Behaviour Research and Therapy, 37,* S53–S77. doi:10.1016/S0005-7967(99)00050-9.

Teasdale, J. D., Segal, Z., & Williams, J. M. (1995). How does cognitive therapy prevent depressive relapse and why should attentional control (mindfulness) training help? *Behaviour Research and Therapy, 33,* 25–39. doi:10.1016/0005-7967(94)E0011-7.

Walach, H., Buchheld, N., Buttenmüller, V., Kleinknecht, N., & Schmidt, S. (2006). Measuring mindfulness—The Freiburg Mindfulness Inventory (FMI). *Personality and Individual Differences, 40,* 1543–1555. doi:10.1016/j.paid.2005.11.025.

Watson, D., Clark, L. A., & Tellegen, A. (1988). Development and validation of brief measures of positive and negative affect: The PANAS scales. *Journal of Personality and Social Psychology, 54,* 1063–1070. doi:10.1037/0022-3514.54.6.1063.

Weintraub, W. (1989). *Verbal behavior in everyday life.* New York, NY: Springer.

CHAPTER SUMMARY

In this article, Scott Lilienfeld (2010) discusses how fear is more often than not an emotion that many people would choose never to experience. Sometimes, "When fears become extreme, they manifest themselves as phobias: intense, irrational apprehension of places, objects, or situations" (p. 16). He continues by articulating how "when fear of public speaking reaches excessive proportions, it becomes a social phobia, also called social anxiety disorder. People with social phobia are petrified of situations in which they could become embarrassed or humiliated" (p. 16). Surprisingly, Lilienfeld provides that, although more than 90% of individuals tasked with delivering a speech do exhibit signs of fear of standing before an audience and speaking, more than 90% of those individuals manage to get up there and get through it.

Similar to some of the biological reactions associated with anxiety, when someone is genuinely frightened, their blood vessels begin to tighten and contract, and their heart rate begins to speed up; this is very similar to the concept of fight-flight-freeze. "Psychologically, fear renders us oversensitive to dangers. By doing so, fear often distorts reality" (p. 17), essentially making the situation seem much worse than it is in some cases.

Always bear in mind that nervousness essentially comes from our mind. It is a reaction to the situation we are in at the time. As such, we can overcome its effects if we think positively, receive training, and enact this training in life situations. Every one of us has within us the power to overcome nervousness, anxiety, and stress. In chapter 5, we discuss ways a public speaker can overcome the nervousness and anxiety related to public speaking.

CHAPTER 5

NERVOUSNESS AND PUBLIC SPEAKING

Previously, we have discussed the intricacies of nervousness and walked through the various components associated with the biology and psychology of anxiety. We also spoke about how to leverage our nervousness and channel it as positive energy, thus showing us the benefits of anxiety and nervousness. In this chapter, we will examine the relationship between nervousness and public speaking and how the various connections between biology and psychology can be understood to enhance our perception of the art of public speaking. In addition, we will examine the topic of management and introduce a few methods for how one can manage the effects of nervousness, particularly when public speaking. Stephen Cohen's reading, "Default Public Speaking Settings," provides us with a deeper understanding of this relationship between nervousness and public speaking.

Let's initiate the conversation by revisiting a concept introduced in chapter 1: public speaking is the number one fear for Americans. Why is this? Take a second, close your eyes, and imagine that you have to give a speech to an audience. How do you feel? Most would report that they feel an overwhelming sense of stress and anxiety, possibly followed by panic and fear. This is simply at the thought of delivering a speech; consider the feeling if you were actually before an audience delivering a speech. As we saw in chapters 3 and 4, there are a variety of components associated with the biology and psychology of nervousness and anxiety. What does this mean for the relationship between nervousness and public speaking?

In the reading for chapter 5, you will learn to understand your own default settings as a public speaker, which will aid in your ability to employ many of the tools discussed in the reading to manage your nervousness while public speaking. We can manage our nervousness by first understanding the relationship between anxiety and public speaking but also by looking at different ways of overcoming our nervousness, such as breathing exercises, manipulation of our eye contact with the audience, and incorporating pauses. These are only a few of the useful strategies presented in this reading.

DEFAULT PUBLIC SPEAKING SETTINGS

by Steven D. Cohen

Each of us has default settings—automatic, pre-programmed behaviors that are comfortable and familiar. For example, when someone sneezes, our typical response is "Bless you." We don't often stop to think about why we say "Bless you." We just say it. After all, saying "Bless you" feels "right." When it comes to public speaking, however, some of our default settings may actually be impeding our ability to make a powerful impact on our listeners.

Let's try an experiment. Put down this book for a moment and clasp your hands together by interlocking your fingers as if you are praying. How does your grip feel? Comfortable, right? Normal, hopefully. Now, unclasp your hands, and clasp your hands together the *other* way, so that the opposite thumb is now on top. How does your grip feel now? A little awkward?

We each have a default way of clasping our hands—a pre-programmed grip that feels "right"—just like we each have default ways of getting dressed in the morning, preparing certain meals, and walking from one place to another. Similarly, we each have default public speaking settings—ingrained ways of communicating and interacting with our audience members.

To become a powerful public speaker, you must identify your default public speaking settings and determine the impact that they are having on your capacity to lead. By getting on the balcony, you will be able to see

Steven D. Cohen, "Default Public Speaking Settings," *Public Speaking: The Path to Success*, pp. 9-14, 157. Copyright © 2011 by Cognella, Inc. Reprinted with permission.

"your own default [ways] of interpreting and responding to events around you ... and gain greater latitude and freedom to respond in new and useful ways."[1]

As you observe yourself from the balcony, make a list of the default public speaking settings that are hindering your ability to speak powerfully. Do you nervously adjust your glasses or run your hands through your hair? Do you say "um" or "uh" every few words? Do you clasp your hands in front of your body or behind your back? Once you identify these default settings, you can begin challenging yourself to adjust them.

It is worth noting that adjusting default public speaking settings isn't an easy process; it's a lot like undergoing an orthodontic procedure to eliminate a gap, straighten crooked teeth, or correct an overbite. The process may take time and the changes may feel uncomfortable for awhile, but most people would agree that the result is well worth the effort.

Although you may have many problematic default public speaking settings, you don't have to adjust them all at once. You can make significant progress by pushing yourself to overcome nervousness, eliminate filler words, and use natural gestures.

OVERCOMING NERVOUSNESS

Most speakers are not naturally at ease in front of an audience. In fact, many people are downright afraid of speaking in public. But when you ask these people why they feel nervous, you quickly learn that they are afraid of what *might* happen. The truth is, most of the preconceived notions that people have about public speaking stem from uncertainty about what their colleagues or friends may think of them after they finish speaking.

The only way to deal with this uncertainty is to step up. You must face any fear that you have, even the fear of being in the spotlight, because public speaking is not really about being in the spotlight. On the contrary, it is about self-sacrifice. It is about using your voice to say something that really matters.

The next time you start to feel nervous, try using a technique called the "T Repeater." Take a deep breath in and then exhale short "T" sounds very slowly until you are out of air. Go ahead. Try it. Breathe in and exhale, "Tuh-Tuh-Tuh-Tuh-Tuh-Tuh-Tuh-Tuh." Focus on relaxing your mind and your shoulders as you are exhaling. Try to make sure that your short "T" sounds are evenly spaced. Feel yourself releasing your nervousness as you let out one short "T" sound after another.

Another technique that you may want to consider is turning your palms up. You tend to be more nervous when your palms are face down next to the sides of your body. If you turn your palms up, you are less likely to have sweaty palms. So before you speak, turn your palms up, breathe in slowly, and then breathe out slowly. Repeat this exercise a few times. Then walk to the front of the room and dazzle your audience.

If you are especially nervous about speaking in front of an audience, you may want to try easing into eye contact. Many speakers believe that they have to look at their audience members right away. In reality, speakers need only create the *impression* that they are looking at their audience members. To create this effect, look at the space between an audience member's eyes or the lower part of her forehead. If there is some space between you and your audience, you also can look at the top of an audience member's head or the rims of his glasses. Shift your eye contact every few seconds just as you would if you were looking directly at individual audience members. You can use this technique until you are comfortable enough to make genuine eye contact with your audience.

Of course, these exercises will only help you overcome your last-minute jitters if you are prepared. Some speakers are nervous when they are getting ready to speak because they are not sure what they are going to say or how their speech is going to turn out. This is why it is so important that you know your material and know it well.

ELIMINATING FILLER WORDS

Once you overcome your nervousness, you will be able to focus on one of the most common default public speaking settings—the use of filler words.

Why do we use filler words? The simplest answer is that we have been conditioned to answer questions immediately from an early age. When our mother or father asked a question, we were sure to answer right away—either because we wanted to show respect or because we were afraid of getting in trouble. Consequently, we feel the urge to speak when spoken to.

Some people argue that filler words are so common in everyday speech that they are generally accepted. But just because filler words may seem "natural" does not mean that they belong in formal speeches. After all, many people find filler words extremely distracting and equate the use of filler words with a lack of preparation or capability. Powerful public speakers work hard to eliminate words such as "um," "uh," "well," "so," "you know," "er," and "like" from their vocabulary so that their listeners are able to focus solely on their message.

There are two places where filler words commonly appear: at the beginning of a statement and in between ideas. See what happens the next time you are asked a question. You probably will say "um" or "uh" right away without even thinking.

Then when you are finished discussing your first idea, you are likely to fill the silence with another filler word before transitioning to your next idea. You can think of these two "filler word hot spots" in the context of a two-paragraph essay. The first hot spot would be the tab before the first paragraph and the second hot spot would be the white space between the first and second paragraphs.

When you use a filler word such as "um," you are thinking verbally. In other words, you are verbalizing your thought process. Armed with this information, it is easy to realize that the best way to avoid using filler words is to *pause*. If you're not speaking, you can't say "um"! Instead of speaking right away, take a couple seconds to think about what you want to say. Then begin speaking. Pause, think, answer.

The same technique applies when you're transitioning from one idea to another. While you may be tempted to fill the silence between ideas with a filler word, remember to pause and give yourself a moment to think about what you want to say next. Don't begin speaking until you are ready. Remember: Pause, think, answer.

It may feel unnatural to pause, especially because you've been thinking aloud for your entire life. I assure you, however, that you will deliver more powerful speeches and reduce your chance of using filler words if you give yourself time to think.

If you need help overcoming a filler word problem, ask a family member, friend, or colleague to point out when you say "um" or "uh." You also may want to wear a rubber band so that you can snap yourself every time you use a filler word. I don't want you to hurt yourself; I want you to stop using filler words!

Although we live in a fast-paced society that seemingly demands instant answers, we must use the pause to our advantage. We may feel pressure to answer right away, but ultimately, we should only speak when we are ready.

USING NATURAL GESTURES

Now that we have discussed a verbal default public speaking setting, let's turn our attention to a common nonverbal setting—the use of distracting hand gestures.

Many speakers default to crossing their arms, playing with their wedding ring, or putting their hands behind their back because they are unsure how to use their hands to their advantage. Although these behaviors may seem harmless, they can dramatically change the way that your audience members interpret your message. If you don't know what to do with your hands, leave them by your sides. But if you want to use your hands to enhance your speech, then you must learn how to gesture naturally.

Gestures are nonverbal extensions of your speech that emphasize the particular ideas that you are sharing verbally. They are important nonverbal tools that narrow the distance between you and your audience. When you reach out toward your audience members, you are physically getting closer to them. You also are conveying your emotions in a more direct and personal way.

Given the importance of gestures, you may feel tempted to insert them at particular points in your speech. However, you shouldn't try to time your gestures. Instead, you must give yourself permission to gesture naturally and purposefully.

In *There's No Such Thing as Public Speaking*, Jeanette and Roy Henderson explain that the best gestures aren't planned:

> When the image is strong enough and the point important enough, your gesture center will automatically provide the uncontrollable urge to gesture, as well as the appropriate gesture to express that image. The best rule of thumb for gestures is simply to just *wait for it*, then when you feel it, *go for it*! Eventually, with experience, you will never need to consciously think about your gestures again.[2]

It is important to feel rather than plan your gestures so that they naturally align with your words. Planned gestures look canned and insincere and often distract your audience members from what you are saying. Give yourself permission to gesture, and you will produce powerful, purposeful gestures every time.

NOTES

1. Ronald Heifetz, Martin Linsky, and Alexander Grashow, *The Practice of Adaptive Leadership: Tools and Tactics for Changing Your Organization and the World* (Boston: Harvard Business Press, 2009), 178.

2. Jeanette Henderson and Roy Henderson, *There's No Such Thing as Public Speaking* (New York: Prentice Hall, 2007), 107.

CHAPTER SUMMARY

Nervousness is an inevitable factor associated with public speaking. It is up to us to understand what this relationship looks like in general as well as for ourselves. As you saw in the reading, we all maintain public speaking tendencies that are unique to us; with the knowledge of what they are and how they influence our ability to speak in public, we can begin to employ various strategies to manage this nervousness and anxiety and strengthen our public speaking capabilities. But the strategies we can incorporate do not end here. In chapter 6, we will examine some unique exercises that can help soothe our anxiety and calm our minds when speaking in public.

CHAPTER 6

MEDITATION AND MINDFULNESS

In the previous chapter, we took a look at the relationship between nervousness and public speaking. Stephen Cohen's reading provided us with insight into what this association looks like and offered various tools for us to incorporate to manage this anxiety. In this chapter, we take a look at concepts associated with mindfulness and their application to the public speaking process. We will also look at how meditation and mindfulness can be used as effective tools, not only to aid in our growth as public speakers but also to decrease stress, regain focus, and become more in tune with ourselves.

In the reading, "Creating the Conditions for Growth and Learning: Mindfulness as a Contribution to Sustainable Learning," Lina Lanestrand provides an in-depth look into the idea of mindfulness and its effective attributes. Meditation and mindfulness were originally concepts derived from religion, but they have more recently been incorporated into the everyday lives of Westerners. The ability to meditate and engage oneself in introspection and self-examination is important for individuals who seek to grow and develop in a general sense: it allows for one to maintain the openness to learning new ideas and engaging in unfamiliar tasks. This reading will walk you through the various components associated with mindfulness and its importance in our lives.

CREATING THE CONDITIONS FOR GROWTH AND LEARNING

MINDFULNESS AS A CONTRIBUTION TO SUSTAINABLE LEARNING

by Lina Lanestrand

Mindfulness is a concept that originated in Buddhist philosophy and is referred to as sati (Plank 2011). Mindfulness is often, in Swedish, translated as awareness of the present moment. In Buddhism, *sati* is a complex term and can be described and interpreted in different ways. *Sati* has been practised for a long time to help people achieve a balanced mind as a way to create a more peaceful world. Sati is practised for instance through meditation and is characterised by approaches like awareness, non-judgment and presence. In the West, mindfulness is applied primarily to help people to manage stress, illness and difficulties in life. The religious and philosophical elements of mindfulness have been removed in the West where it is used as a tool in our busy lives.

The qualitative study *Mindfulness—learning processes in awareness of the presence* (Lanestrand 2012) is based on three narrative written stories and five deep narrative interviews with people who practice mindfulness

Lina Lanestrand, "Creating the Conditions for Growth and Learning: Mindfulness as a Contribution to Sustainable Learning," *Social Alternatives*, vol. 31, no. 4, pp. 58-61. Copyright © 2012 by Social Alternatives. Reprinted with permission. Provided by ProQuest LLC. All rights reserved.

in their everyday life. Six of the participants are trained mindfulness instructors. The study is the basis for this article and demonstrates that mindfulness, from a pedagogical perspective, is a learning process with an ethical dimension that creates space. If education involves mindfulness as a way to create the best conditions for learning it can contribute to sustainable learning. But this can be quite radical. Jacques Ranciére (1991) for instance argues that education has a hidden agenda, which makes people and pupils believe that they cannot learn and educate themselves. Mindfulness is a powerful tool that enables the learner to experience connection with oneself, our ability to develop and learn, which can contribute to emancipating people.

The mindful space explored in my study found that mindfulness provides room for individual contact with oneself, contact with others, contact with existential and spiritual aspects of life, as well as a deeper experience of time that allows for moments or spaces in time that foster re-perceiving, a shift in perspective. This multiple space provides room for our human abilities to learn and grow. The actual learning process of mindfulness has parallels with John Dewey's (2009) concept of *learning by doing*. Hence, developing mindfulness is achieved through experiences, insights and the practice of meditation and mindfulness-based exercises.

Individual experience is central to mindfulness yet Dewey (2009) states that experience can have both passive and active elements. The active part involves making experiences while the passive means going through something and finding oneself in a situation/experience *as it is*. Such learning 'as-it-is' also means to accept the consequences that arise from our actions. Dewey notes:

> When we experience something we observe it and we do something with it, then we suffer or endure the consequences. We do something about the conditions and then they do something to us in return, such is the specific combination (Dewey 2009: 183).

A change is created, according to Dewey, when we progress from having done something to experiencing the consequences that this causes and internalising this change within ourselves. This inner change also gives the event a meaning, and that is what happens when we learn something. Dewey exemplifies this with a child burning her finger in a candle flame. The external change, the burning of the finger, is only relevant when it is linked with the previous action (putting the finger in the flame) and when it is connected with the significance (of pain) that the child experienced—then there is learning. Dewey argues that learning through experience involves both body and mind and is both active and passive.

> ... the only way to understand what is meant by direct experience of something is to have it yourself (2009: 282).

All participants in the study (Lanestrand 2012) expressed precisely what Dewey (2009) describes, namely that mindfulness can only be fully understood through one's own experience. This means that mindfulness is difficult to define fully with just words. There is an embodied and solitary dimension to this kind of understanding. Ranciére (1991) explains that the learning that you do by yourself, without explanations, is a universal learning. This has parallels with Dewey's (2009) learning by doing because both focus on learning by oneself from life itself and our own experience.

MINDFULNESS CREATES CONDITIONS FOR GROWING

The results of the study (Lanestrand 2012) demonstrate that participants who continually apply mindfulness as part of their everyday lives experience positive changes. These changes mean that they can manage life, themselves and other people better. Furthermore they experience life as richer than before. These results match many other different scientific studies of mindfulness (Plank 2011). As participants described the effects of mindfulness in their daily lives the connections to Dewey's (2009) philosophy became clearer.

Dewey sees immaturity as one prerequisite for human learning and development. Immaturity is a complex term, since it has negative connotations. Potential is perhaps a better term—as it conveys the possibility of growing and learning. The term immaturity corresponds well, however, with some of the approaches applied in mindfulness such as curiosity and beginner's mind. This approach means having an open mind and being curious about each new encounter and situation (including with yourself) while refraining from having ready answers and automatic reactions.

Dewey (2009) argues that our view of immaturity affects our view of learning. Immaturity is often regarded as a deficiency, which leads to the risk that education and development are used to correct this deficiency, so that the child achieves 'maturity'. Adults are considered to be mature and this establishes a norm around 'adultness'. This has the consequence that opportunities and abilities in the present are likely to be underestimated and overlooked. It is important to recognise that both adults and children are in a constant process of learning and growing and that development occurs under various conditions. Ultimately Dewey believes that growing itself is life and writes:

> ... life is development, and to develop, to grow is life (ibid: 88).

Accordingly, development ceases when it is replaced by passive adaptation. For him learning itself is always the goal, the content learnt is of secondary consideration.

> Growing is considered too easily as something that has a goal rather than being a goal (ibid: 89).

To understand learning in this we come to appreciate that life itself is about learning and that the role of mindful attention is to deepen our ongoing learning journeys. Such a perspective accepts all life as of unique value and creates a non-violent learning space from which the questions of sustainability arise. In this way mindfulness can contribute to forms of holistic education that involve new perspectives on learning, human beings and life, as well as nature.

MINDFULNESS AS PROCESS

Participants in the study support Dewey's position. They described mindfulness as a process, a journey without a goal. As one participant noted:

> Mindfulness is a continuous journey, constantly, without goals, mindfulness is something that is constantly evolving, and life really is so rich and has so many dimensions. A journey of discovery, without specific goals, it's about living life as full as possible and to take advantage of the moments and the resources you have, not only for yourself but also for others (Lanestrand 2012: 40).

Thus mindfulness itself becomes an example of engaged-learning, where the learning process itself is essential. Such a perspective challenges conventional learning models, which push children to meet a uniform outcome. This implicit goal often means that children should be as adults. This results in the uniqueness and individuality of each person being suppressed and the love of learning being killed. Instead, external factors such as reward and punishment are used to achieve the desired outcome. To challenge this mindful education creates the conditions for the desire to learn directly from life itself.

Ranciére (1991) helps us here as he writes about how we all learn our native language by ourselves, without any explanations. He argues that the will to learn emerges from the context in which the child resides. The context itself draws forth the learning:

> The method of equality was above all a method of the will. One could learn by oneself and without a master explicator when one wanted to, propelled by one's own desire or by the constraint of the situation (Ranciére 1991: 12).

Ranciére also notes that a child only needs a master when her own will is weak or when she is having problems getting on her own track. For Ranciére (1991) this suggests a core principle of universal teaching:

> One must learn something and relate everything else to it (1991: 20).

Perhaps this is what sustainable learning itself means: to be empowered to learn from your own interest, by your own will and to learn by doing and to create context and meaningfulness?

MINDFULNESS IS SLOW

All participants (Lanestrand, 2012) refer in different ways to the child's spontaneous and natural way of being in the present. One of the participants stated that as children we are all in the core of ourselves, alive to the present, but that as we grow we put a lid on who we are. When confronting this 'lid' we will experience pain because it prevents us from being in direct contact with ourselves. For learning to be sustainable and foster sustainable life habits this lid needs to be challenged.

Dewey writes that it is important to be understood as the one you are, to be seen and appreciated for it, which is a prerequisite for being able to do and contribute to society.

> If you never will be understood or appreciated for who you are, you lose some of your ability to be a resource for other goals (2009: 289).

All participants (Lanestrand, 2012) testify that the application of mindfulness awakens this ability to grow and develop as a person. From Dewey's perspective mindfulness is something that relieves adults from the burden of their maturity and instead gives life to their immaturity; or put more simply—mindfulness awakens their developmental potential. It is clear that mindfulness can help us to deal with questions about sustainability in a new way. Orr (2002) writes that we need to start from where we are.

> For most of us the Great Work must begin where we are, in the small acts of everyday life, stitching together a pattern of loyalty and faithfulness to a higher order of being (2002: 5).

To be able to begin where we are, we need to mindfully pay attention to ourselves in the moment. Then we can take new steps in sustainability development.

Orr also talks about fast and slow knowledge. He argues that fast knowledge has terrible consequences for human beings, animals, and nature.

> But many, if not most, of the ecological, economic, social, and psychological ailments that beset contemporary society can be attributed directly or indirectly to knowledge acquired and applied before we had time to think it through carefully. (ibid: 37)

He continues this line of argument stating that the consequences of fast knowledge are deferred to the future.

> The result is that the system of fast knowledge creates social traps in which the benefits occur in the near term while the costs are deferred to others at a later time (ibid: 40).

A learning in mindfulness, as characterised by consciousness and presence, promotes the slow and can contribute to sustainable learning, where nonviolence, compassion and responsibility are natural parts of knowledge not measured in speed.

A SUSTAINABLE LEARNING

There is broad consensus on the need for further research on mindfulness. In the wealth of studies presented today about mindfulness, there are a number of deficiencies (Lanestrand, 2012). There is a lack of an agreed definition of what mindfulness really is (Plank, 2011). Many studies seem unclear as to what they actually seek to measure and study. In short the view of what mindfulness is varies depending on who the viewer is.

In my study (2012) I conclude with an attempt to describe mindfulness as a pedagogical tool. I see mindfulness as a learning process in awareness of the present with ethical dimensions beyond the utilitarian, which are characterised by learning through experience and sensation, combined with reflection and insight.

Langer (1997) uses the term mindful learning as a description of learning characterised by an open and inquisitive mind. Such a mind is innovative and aware that there is not only one correct answer. Langer echoes Dewey's (2009) criticism of the pedagogy in schools and education. Although they were writing at different times, they describe the same deficiencies. Both Ranciére and Dewey (2009) state that children are disempowered when they are forced to study educational content that they have no interest in; Langer (1997) argues that finished truths are delivered to children and that as a result there is often a lack of commitment and motivation in schools.

Following Ranciére's argument nobody can really tell you all about mindfulness, you need to experience it yourself. And when you do, you experience it as self-awareness. In this way mindfulness contributes to sustainable learning, because it empowers people—when they learn how to learn by themselves to be themselves. In this way mindfulness contributes to our human potential with approaches and tools in educational contexts, to create conditions for a sustainable and truly empowering learning. Thus mindfulness:

- Makes us aware of the present, which is the only time we can be in—in the present we cannot run from the past nor hide in the future—instead we can develop responsibility and sustainability, here and now.

- Helps us feel the context and the wholeness, instead of separating life into parts.

- Helps us to connect to the value, the richness and happiness of life, which can give us the power and energy to handle sustainability challenges.

- Connects to ourselves so we can know our own will and use it as a base for our own learning and development as humans.

- Develops empathy with other people, which can lead to a wholeness and feeling of empathy and responsibility with people all around the world.

- Creates a learning climate characterised by self-awareness, which can help us see the consequences of our actions.

- Empowers people when they learn how to learn things by themselves.

- Reduces stress and strengthens health—which can help us feel better in body and soul, and make better decisions.

A sustainable learning is sustainable for the individual—where learning itself is the goal and the learning starts from the individual, extends to the community and where it fosters resilience and inclusivity. I argue that mindfulness in education can help teachers and children connect to one another and most importantly find their inner learning space and connection with their own potential. Of course mindfulness itself is not the only solution yet it can start a new kind of process in education—one which can lead to increased sustainability. Through the application of mindfulness in research, teaching and education there is clearly an opportunity for the development of a mindful and sustainable pedagogy.

REFERENCES

Brown, K. Ryan, R Cresswell, D. 2007, *Mindfulness: Theoretical Foundations and Evidence for its Salutary Effect*, http://www.kirkwarrenbrown.vcu.edu/wpcontent/pubs/Brown%20et%20al%20PI%202007.pdf, accessed on 28th May 2012.

Dewey, J. 2009, *Democracy and Education*, Daidalos, Gothenburg.

Langer, E. 1997, *The power of mindful learning*, Da Capo Press, Cambridge.

Lanestrand, L. 2012, *Mindfulness—learning processes in awareness of the presence*, Södertörn University http://linalanestrand.se/wp-content/uploads/2012/06/Mindfulness-lärprocesser-i-medveten-närvaro.-20121.pdf.

Orr, D. 2002, *The Nature of Design. Ecology, Culture and Human Intention*, Oxford Unity, New York.

Plank, K. 2011, *Insight and Attendance: Academic Contemplations about Buddhism, Meditation and Mindfulness*, Scandinavian Book, Århus.

Ranciére, J. 1991, The Ignorant Schoolmaster, Stanford University Press, Stanford.

Shapiro, S.L. Carlson, L.E. Astin, JA & Freedman, B. 2006, 'Mechanisms of mindfulness', *Journal of Clinical Psychology*, Vol. 62(3) pp. 373–386.

Walsch, N. 1995, *Conversations with God*, Richter, Malmö.

AUTHOR

Lina Lanestrand is a pedagogue, writer and food-inspirer, currently working part-time as an organisational developer in health promotion at Riksförbundet Hälsofrämjandet www.halsoframjandet.se. Lina also runs the company www.linalanestrand.se with her husband, in which she gives courses and speeches about health and lifestyle. Lina is very interested in sustainable development and their company distributes locally grown organic vegetables in western Sweden. Lina previously worked with human rights and children's rights with the nongovernmental organisation Save the Children, in Sweden. Lina has a focus on all children's right to be involved in areas of life that affect them. She is currently creating a national adult education programme, sponsored by Save the Children Sweden, which focuses on the child's right to be heard. The main issue in this is to help adults to really listen and to be truly present with kids.

CHAPTER SUMMARY

As can be seen, mindfulness fosters an environment that is accepting of overall human growth and development. As public speakers, we are constantly growing and cultivating our skills as effective communicators. Through the use of meditation, we are able to center and ground ourselves, regain control over our breathing, and place ourselves into a more positive mindset. With the use of the concepts offered through mindfulness, we are able to look within ourselves and examine our current abilities as public speakers and our apprehensions associated with the task and to be more open-minded to utilizing tools to strengthen our public speaking capabilities. In our next chapter, we discuss confidence and its role in public speaking.

CHAPTER 7
BUILDING CONFIDENCE

Previously, we spoke about the idea of using meditation to control our breathing and align our mindset with a more positive outlook on public speaking. Additionally, we examined the concepts of mindfulness and how being in tune with oneself allows us to engage in overall growth and development, not only as a public speaker but also as an individual in society. In this chapter, we are looking at confidence and its association with public speaking. To say "Have confidence in yourself" may be easier said than done, but with the tools provided in Paul R. Timm's and Sherron Bienvenu's reading, "Deliver Your Message with Confidence and Impact," we are able to strengthen our understanding of confidence and employ it in our public speaking opportunities.

DELIVER YOUR MESSAGE WITH CONFIDENCE AND IMPACT

by Paul R. Timm and Sherron Bienvenu

There are four things people you communicate with won't forgive you for: not being prepared, comfortable, committed, and interesting.

(Roger Ailes, *You Are the Message*)

DELIVERING YOUR MESSAGES

Many people experience some anxiety when speaking before others. In public speaking, this anxiety is often quite significant. But even in less-formal situations such as giving a briefing or leading a meeting—or even participating in an interview—anxiety can play a significant part in inhibiting effectiveness.

Communicators who fail to consider the delivery part of their communication efforts run the risk of having their carefully planned messages fall flat.

This chapter discusses the steps necessary to deliver your message content in ways that maximize its impact on your audience.

Paul R. Timm and Sherron Bienvenu, "Deliver Your Message with Confidence and Impact," *Straight Talk: Oral Communication for Career Success*, pp. 138-167, 269. Copyright © 2011 by Taylor & Francis Group. Reprinted with permission.

PERFORMANCE COMPETENCIES

When you have completed this chapter, you should be able to:

- Polish your delivery using appropriate verbal, non-verbal, and platform-management skills.

- Speak clearly and expressively, pay attention to timing, avoid distracting vocal patterns, and minimize verbalized pauses.

- Manage notes and visual aids comfortably, and handle audience questions succinctly.

- Maintain eye contact, dress professionally, exhibit physical control, and project enthusiasm.

- Express confidence through an understanding of your material and your audience's needs.

- Appreciate the importance of being yourself and continuing to improve your delivery skills.

THE WAY IT IS ... COMMUNICATING ON THE NEW JOB

Brenda Flores was both excited and anxious about her management position with a high-tech multi-national corporation. As an engineer, Brenda had contributed to the design and development of several important, successful products. And now, her division had undergone a major re-organization at the very top level that had resulted in the appointment of a new vice-president.

Brenda had heard that the new VP was just one indication of a new corporate focus on her division, and she expected that there would be a larger budget and more opportunities for upward mobility. That was the exciting part.

Brenda had also heard that this new VP placed a high priority not only on smart people with good solutions, but also on those who could engage an audience and present their ideas with professional style. He expected his team to "step up and speak up."

Brenda was comfortable in small meetings with other engineers, but she never had to actually stand up and present there. She did well making a point in a limited time, but she always depended on notes and numbers. And even though she thought of herself as Senior Manager material, she realized she didn't sound as confident or look as "put together" as the people in the level ahead of her. The thought of having to "give a speech" or even to speak up in a meeting in front of her new boss pretty much terrified her. The more she thought about it, the more she questioned her ability to move ahead.

Everybody worries a bit about communicating in front of others. People want others to think well of them; they care about how effective they are being and sincerely want others to get their messages. They want to participate in group decisions and offer suggestions and ideas. And employers want people who do exactly those kinds of things. A company's most valuable people are those who communicate well.

[...] Specifically in this chapter, we will concentrate on five key factors necessary to deliver effective oral messages:

- Polishing your verbal delivery skills.

- Developing your platform-management skills.

- Polishing your non-verbal delivery skills.

- Showing confidence and enthusiasm.

- Rehearsing and editing.

- Managing anxiety and expressing confidence.

- Being yourself and becoming your better self.

THE WIDESPREAD USE OF ORAL COMMUNICATION IN THE WORKPLACE

Oral communication in business is widespread and often takes the form of presentations. When you plan, prepare, and create a message to deliver to others, you make a presentation. Presentations vary in their degree of formality, but all are purposeful communication aimed at achieving a specific result. These are not speeches, although a speech can be one form of presentation. We are using the term to denote something broader. The following are some examples of presentations common in businesses:

- Alan Harris explains service department bills to his auto-repair customers. He communicates what work was done, why it was done, and how much it cost. Alan makes presentations.

- Heidi Astin sells upscale automobiles at a mid-size Porsche dealership. She greets customers, provides technical information, encourages test drives, advises on financing options, and handles all facets of these big-ticket sales. Heidi makes presentations.

- Michelle Harker serves as a facilities manager overseeing nine buildings for a rapidly expanding regional bank, She reports regularly to the bank's executive committee describing progress on new construction, remodeling, and maintenance issues. She shares her expertise and recommends the best office options for the company's needs. Michelle makes presentations.

- Carol Tanaka is searching for a new job, one that makes the most of her recently completed MBA. She has interviews almost every day and works hard to sell her talents and skills to prospective employers. Carol makes presentations.

- Carl Steinburg is having a performance appraisal with his boss today. He feels good about his work accomplishments and hopes to be considered for a promotion. Carl will make a presentation.

- Eric Jessop represents his company in community-service efforts that teach young people how to avoid drugs, alcohol, and relationship problems. Eric makes presentations.

- Marin Pickard has a highly responsible position in business development for an aircraft manufacturer. She represents both the company and its products to influential clients across the globe. Marin makes presentations.

- Charles Dunwoody is a Human Resources Manager who participates in decision-making meetings involving personnel issues from staffing to the results of employee surveys. Charles makes presentations.

"Hold it a second," you may be saying. "It's beginning to sound like *everything* people do is some form of a presentation." Well, that's about right. We all spend a large portion of our lives making presentations—offering information, persuading, or giving bad news to others. That is the reality of the work world.

Most communication activities can be viewed as "making presentations."

POLISH YOUR VERBAL DELIVERY SKILLS

Your specific audiences and the culture of your business will help shape the decisions you make about your communication style over the course of your career. As you speak and observe the reactions to your speaking, you will learn appropriate responses and make adjustments that become your personalized style. Some generic guidelines for success—some tricks and some common mistakes to avoid—can also be helpful in polishing your delivery skills.

Your verbal skills go beyond the words you choose. They also include the way you use your voice—pronunciation, articulation, volume, and pitch—and the dramatic aspects—emphasis, pace, and timing. In other words, verbal skills include how you use words to speak clearly and expressively. In the following sections we will look at ways in which you can improve your verbal skills.

Message delivery goes beyond the words of the message.

SPEAK CLEARLY

Concentrate on improving your pronunciation, articulation, volume, and pitch so that your audience can easily and comfortably hear and understand your words. Pronounce words correctly. Replace just one "pitcher" for "picture," and you will lose credibility with your audience. Articulate your words. Say all the letters in all the syllables of every word. Don't relax into "lemme" for "let me" or "gonna" for "going to."

Adjust the volume of your voice to your audience. Don't speak so loudly that you sound like an orator—like an old-fashioned pitchman on a soapbox. But don't speak so softly that you sound insecure or lacking in enthusiasm either. One myth is that if you speak quietly, an audience will lean in to hear you. The truth is that if you speak too softly, your audience is likely to go to sleep. Instead, simply direct your talk toward the people farthest from you. This focus will help you increase your volume.

Use variation in volume as well as in other vocal qualities such as pitch and rate of speech. Sameness becomes monotonous; variation attracts and holds people's attention and interest. Psychologists say that no one can pay attention to an unchanging stimulus for very long. We can't watch grass grow or paint dry. It's just too boring. Unfortunately, speakers who insist on using never-changing vocal patterns sound just about as boring.

Vocal variation (of pitch, rate, and volume) helps hold listener attention.

SPEAKING AT A LOWER PITCH

In many cultures, adults sound more credible when they speak using a lower pitch. To find the lowest pitch that is comfortable for you, try this: lie flat on your back and relax. Breathe from your diaphragm without moving your shoulders (this is easier to learn while lying down than while standing up). Then read out loud. The pitch you hear is your natural pitch. Try to maintain the same sound when you are standing up by simply relaxing and breathing from your diaphragm. Do not, however, maintain this pitch monotonously. The idea is to speak naturally, just a little lower, and with more resonance.

SPEAK EXPRESSIVELY

Work to perfect your emphasis and pace so that your audience can easily understand the meaning of your words. When you outline your presentations and practice your delivery, determine which words are the most important and then underline or highlight those words in your notes. Which words you emphasize can change the meaning of your sentences. Think of the different inflections you could give the question, "What do you mean by that?"

- *What* do you mean by that?

- What *do* you mean by that?

- What do *you* mean by that?

- What do you *mean* by that?

- What do you mean by *that*?

You can hear how different emphasis changes the sentence's implications and meaning. Be sensitive to implications of various inflections. The above examples can sound inquisitive or accusatory, depending on the emphasis. Perhaps your listeners will hear these "hidden meanings."

Let's try one more example. Put the emphasis on a different word in this simple statement:

- *I* think Maryanne can do that (but no one else thinks so).

- I *think* Maryanne can do that (maybe she can).

- I think *Maryanne* can do that (she could, but no one else can).

- I think Maryanne *can* do that (she could but may not want to).

- I think Maryanne can do *that* (she can't do much else, but that she can do).

Emphasis on a different word can change the implied message of even a simple statement.

Many speakers get feedback that indicates that they talk too fast; some talk too slowly. But trying to slow down quick-speak may seem awkward, as can trying to speed up a deliberative, slower pace.

If you tend to speak quickly (some cultures encourage this), consider this. A better alternative may be to identify material that is new, difficult, unusual, or particularly important for the audience and focus on presenting that information at a slower pace. Then return to your comfortable, normal, faster pace. Again, you may want to highlight this important information on your outline.

The challenge of speaking too slowly is that people listen faster than you can deliver the message. Their minds go ahead of you and may jump to unintended conclusions. It can be difficult to listen to 120 spoken words a minute when your brain is thinking at 500 wpm. You simply have too much "free time" to let the mind wander.

Speaking too slowly can be just as distracting as speaking too fast—perhaps more so.

PAY ATTENTION TO TIMING

One of the most dramatic effects a speaker can learn to use is timing. The pause can be a powerful emphasis tool. There are many places a pause can enhance your presentation:

- After you walk to the front of the room but before you begin speaking.

- Before you make an important point ("This is the bottom line:" [pause]).

- After you make an important point ("Our profits would be in the millions [pause] if we …").

- When you ask a question (pausing may feel awkward; however, most speakers don't wait long enough).

- As a transition between main points ("That sums up the problem." [pause] "We are looking at several solutions.").

- After your final statement and before "Thank you."

The rate of speech can either help or hinder the listener. Go slowly enough to get the ideas across, but not so slow that listeners "fill in the blanks" or wander off.

SPEAKING WITH AN ACCENT

Do you think that you have an accent that distracts your audience and diminishes the perception of your credibility? Well, everyone has an accent! We all have a vocal signature. If you are from a geographical location that is unique to your workgroup, you might sound different from them. Or, if the language you are using is not your native tongue, you will sound different from native speakers.

Typically, your accent or even your sentence structure and vocabulary, which might be different, are not the problem. Audiences are open to such variations in today's global business environment. A mild accent can be charming—*unless* your audience has trouble understanding you. Then we recommend one basic tactic: *articulate all of the syllables in all of your words*. Focusing on articulation will also slow you down and give your audience time to become accustomed to your rhythm. Soon, your accent will be one reason why you are unique and engaging—and it will no longer be a distraction.

AVOID DISTRACTING VOCAL PATTERNS

Some speakers get into voice patterns that undermine their professionalism. Speakers who let the end of sentences trail off into a soft mumble are one such example. Another distracting vocal pattern is what is called "up-speak." Here the speaker raises intonation at the end of a statement, making it sound like a question. Say the following sentences aloud using up-speak—raising intonation on the italicized word—and you'll hear how this can undermine a message.

- She's very good at everything she *does*. (The listener will ask: "Is she?")

- The management is concerned about the *costs*. (The listener will ask: "Are they?")

- My name is John *Mansfield*. (The listener will ask: "Are you sure?")

Notice how up-speak creates a note of uncertainty in what is spoken. Unfortunately, some people habitually use up-speak without noticing how it can undermine their assertiveness and make them consistently sound tentative.

Up-speak creates a sense of uncertainty and can undermine your credibility. You will sound less confident when your statements sound like questions.

MINIMIZE VERBALIZED PAUSES

Few things can drive an audience crazy like the liberal use of verbalized fillers, such as "ah," "um," "uh," and (a popular favorite) "ya know." Some intelligent and apparently rational men and women salt their every utterance with these expressions until their listeners want to scream at them, *ya know*?

The human talker abhors a vacuum. When the detested monster, silence, raises its ugly head, some beat it to death with "ah," "uh," "um," or "ya know." Do yourself a favor: ask someone you trust to point out when you are drifting into this habit. Commit yourself to listening for and eliminating your own filler words. Rid yourself of the fear of silence.

FILLER WORD USE[1]

Why do some people fill the air with non-words and sounds? For some, it is a sign of nervousness; they fear silence and experience speaker anxiety. Recent research at Columbia University suggests another reason. Columbia psychologists speculated that speakers fill pauses when searching for the next word. To investigate this idea, they counted the use of filler words used by lecturers in biology, chemistry, and mathematics, where the subject matter uses scientific definitions that limit the variety of word choices available to the speaker.

They then compared the number of filler words used by teachers in English, art history, and philosophy, where the subject matter is less well-defined and more open to word choices. Twenty science lecturers used an average of 1.39 uh's a minute, compared with 4.85 uh's a minute by 13 humanities teachers. Their conclusion: subject matter and breadth of vocabulary may determine use of filler words more than habit or anxiety.

Whatever the reason, the cure for filler words is preparation. You reduce nervousness and pre-select the right ways to say ideas through preparation and practice.

DEVELOP YOUR PLATFORM-MANAGEMENT SKILLS

As a speaker, one of your tasks is to manage the communication process. Two aspects of platform management include the careful use of notes and visual aids and the handling of audience interaction, especially question-and-answer (Q&A) opportunities. Work to achieve professionalism in these tasks, which we will discuss in the following sections. (Again, we note that your "platform" may not be a formal speech, but these principles apply to all oral-communication situations.)

USE YOUR NOTES CAREFULLY

If possible, avoid using notes altogether when delivering your message—just use your visuals. Well-prepared visual aids provide a useful set of notes for your presentation. You should be familiar enough with your topic to rely almost entirely on the outline on your visual aids. If you are using a laptop computer, simply turn the screen toward yourself and you will have your "notes" right there.

However, you may need additional notes when:

- Your material is new or too complex to show using just visual aids.

- Visual aids are not appropriate, such as when you are introducing someone or giving a luncheon speech.

- You need to emphasize certain, specific words or concepts, and precise wording is imperative.

In such cases, we suggest writing key words or phrases on note cards that you can carry easily and unobtrusively. If you use note cards, be sure to write only key words (the fewer the better!) in large letters on the cards. Also use cards that are at least 5 × 8; don't try to hide them from your audience.

Note cards are rarely necessary when you use visual aids.

As we have said, the biggest preparation mistake a speaker can make is to write a presentation word-for-word. If you write it, chances are you will read it. Reading a manuscript, no matter how well-written, will negate the positive effects of all your other work on your presentation. You will appear unprepared and unprofessional, and you will severely diminish your chances for success. The only exceptions to this may be in high-level negotiations or when presenting a carefully worded public announcement where a misstatement could create legal difficulties. Dignitaries in delicate negotiation situations may read a prepared speech, too. But such situations are rare in workplace communication.

Corporate executives often have so many speaking engagements that they employ trusted assistants or professional speechwriters to prepare their remarks. Sometimes, this is acceptable. However, it is never okay to read every word. Even the most script-dependent speaker can learn and then just say the first sentence and the last one. No-one needs to read, "Good morning and welcome to Big Corp" or "Thank you so much for coming, and please enjoy your tour of our facility."

If you choose to use handouts, determine if you want the audience to follow along with you as you speak, or if your handouts are for later reference. If the handouts cover additional material or follow a different order than your presentation, distribute them afterwards.

MANAGE YOUR VISUAL AIDS

Your objective with visual aids is to convince your audience that you are the one in control. Your visual aids should not appear to be managing you (like the dog who "walks" the owner). First, be sure your slides look right on the screen and confirm that any embedded sound or video will play. Then, learn to work your equipment. Know, for example, how to move back to your previous slide. Use a remote mouse yourself (thus avoiding the dreaded, "Next slide, please"). If you need a flipchart, check for fresh markers.

Manage your use of visual aids. They can be a source of distraction rather than a help in getting your message across.

When you are presenting, focus on your audience, not on your visual aids. Avoid facing the screen, either reading the slides or talking to them (both look very unprofessional). You may turn and gesture toward the screen to draw your audience's attention to a bullet point or illustration, but immediately turn your face and body back toward your audience. Or, better yet, have your slides displayed on a laptop facing you.

If you can, and if the room allows, stand to the audience's left of your visual aids so their focus is first on you and then on your visual aids. Almost every culture reads from left to right, and after we blink or look down, we automatically look to the left first. Remember, you are most important; your visual aids are just that—aids to support you and your message.

HANDLE QUESTIONS CONSTRUCTIVELY

You should consider two platform-management issues regarding questions: when to take them and how to answer them. Planning the "when" part makes the "how" part easier. We will discuss these issues in the following sections.

WHEN TO ANSWER QUESTIONS

Some speakers feel that they lose control of the situation when the Q&A section starts, so they avoid it as long as possible, in hopes that time will run out. We advise a different strategy. First, tell your audience when you are going to take questions during your presentation. If you are comfortable with interruptions, encourage them, but be aware that you are likely to be interrupted with a question about something that you are planning to cover later in the presentation. When that happens, you either have to jump ahead in your organization (not the best solution) or tell the questioner that you will address the material soon.

Most speakers are better off announcing that they will take questions at the end of each section or at the end of their presentation. This avoids the problem of having the presentation organization thrown off, and gives you the opportunity to answer most of the questions that would have come up.

Second, decide exactly when you will ask for questions at the end. You have two choices: before your summary or after your summary. Either time is fine, based on your personal preference and style. However, do not wait until after your final statement to ask for questions. If you do, you run the risk that the last question asked will be the one that is awkward for you to answer, and that will then be your final impression on your audience. Instead, tell your audience something like this: "I'll take one last question, and then I have a final thought to leave with you."

If you take questions after your summary, you might want to briefly summarize again, perhaps enhancing that summary with issues you addressed in your Q&A. But always leave the audience with a strong, carefully rehearsed final word. [...]

Always keep control of your final statement. Don't end on a Q&A.

HOW TO ANSWER QUESTIONS

Entire books have been written on strategies for answering questions. The basic plan, however, is comprised of three simple steps:

1. Answer the question directly.
2. Offer one piece of support or elaboration.
3. Stop.

Avoid the most common mistake that speakers make when answering questions: they go on and on. Make your point and stop talking. Less is more. If the questioner needs more information, he or she will ask for it. So memorize the three steps: answer, support, stop.

Don't try to bluff. If you don't know the answer to a question, say so. It's perfectly fine—actually, it's preferred—to just say, "I don't know." Then follow up with a comment about finding the answer and getting back to the person who asked the question—if you really intend to do so.

Of course, sometimes you will have to respond to a question that requires more than the "answer, support, stop" plan. Try these tactics:

- Just answer the question directly.

- Rephrase the question ("What I understand that you are asking me is . . .").

- Use the bad-news organizational pattern.

- Defer to someone else ("Joe is the expert . . .").

- Steer the question with a bridge ("What's most important is . . .").

However you choose to answer your questions, just remember to plan the material for afterwards. Your audience will remember your final words.

> *The most common mistake in dealing with listener questions is to rattle on rather than answering the question efficiently.*

POLISH YOUR NON-VERBAL DELIVERY SKILLS

Your non-verbal skills include how you look and how you move. Obviously, you should take your cues from your target audience and your organization, but some fundamental non-verbal abilities are essential. Among these are eye contact, professional appearance, physical control, and enthusiasm, which we will discuss in the following sections.

ESTABLISH AND MAINTAIN EYE CONTACT

In business situations in Western cultures, we expect speakers to look at us when delivering a message. Speakers who do not look us in the eye are regarded as insecure or untrustworthy. When addressing groups, the best way to maintain eye contact is to look at one individual for a few seconds and then move on to another person. Don't just scan over the audience— really *look* at individuals. Try to get to everyone in the room, and be aware of tendencies to look too much at some people and not enough at others. (Some speakers tend to look to one side of a room more than another. Avoid this tendency.)

> *Look directly at each member of your audience.*

DEVELOP AND DISPLAY A PROFESSIONAL IMAGE

Appearance, dress, and grooming communicate powerful messages. Your audience will make some assumptions about you and your message based on how you look. If you aren't sure how to dress for a particular presentation, you are better off being dressed too formally than too informally. Success experts encourage people to dress as if they were at the next level in the organization. If your next promotion is to Director level, then dress like a Director. You can often enhance your credibility by dressing just a bit sharper than the audience expects.

Avoid wearing something that may be distracting.

Don't wear anything that is distracting. In business contexts, men should avoid ties with odd patterns or belt buckles with unusual designs. If you are short, stout, or tend to gesture broadly, you should not wear a double-breasted jacket that makes you look wider and constricts arm movement. Women should not wear things that move or make noise (such as dangling earrings or charm bracelets). They should generally avoid bright nail polish or unusual make-up colors that distract their audience. If you ever find yourself tugging at anything, then you know what to fix next time. (For example, if your hair falls in your face, either cut it or fasten it back.)

Many excellent books and magazine articles can provide dress and grooming tips. Stay current with what is acceptable for the business environment in which you work. But the simplest rule of thumb is to avoid dress or grooming that may distract your listeners from your message.

PROFESSIONAL IMAGE MATTERS ALL THE TIME

As part of the reorganization of a major business unit, senior management was considering the future of one relatively small facility. The General Manager (GM) and his management team at the facility spent several weeks preparing a selection of options and detailing support material. One option was to close the facility altogether; another was to relocate. A less financially attractive, but more personnel-attractive, option was to remain open as a Center for Excellence. Complicating the issue was the fact that the ultimate decision would be made by a new senior vice-president (SVP) who had only visited the site one time and who knew very few of the people involved.

On the day of the decision-making meeting, the facility's GM was completely prepared. He was also dressed in his best suit and had practiced his presentation using the technology in the SVP's conference room. In addition, the GM brought a secret weapon: his entire management team. They, too, were completely prepared and dressed in their best business suits. Sitting in a line at the wall of the conference room, they presented an impressive professional image.

The SVP was apparently influenced. He decided to keep the facility and its people. Did the united force of the team's professional image make an impression? We'll never know for sure, but we do know that it surely didn't hurt.

EXHIBIT PHYSICAL CONTROL

Your sense of personal dynamism or self-confidence comes across via body language such as gestures, posture, and mannerisms. Gestures can be useful to punctuate the message. For example, a pause with a shift in body position can be the non-verbal equivalent of a new paragraph or line of reasoning. Your body movements should be comfortable and natural, yet purposeful.

Make body movements purposeful, not random.

GESTURE SPONTANEOUSLY AND NATURALLY

Everyone has different tendencies to use or avoid gestures. For some, it feels uncomfortable to point or raise hands in exclamation. For others, it may appear that if you tied their hands, they'd be speechless.

The most effective hand gestures are in what is called the "honor zone." This is the area between your waist and shoulders and is where people expect to see gestures. Common mistakes people make with gestures include:

- Failing to use enough gestures.

- Repeating the same gesture to the point where it becomes monotonous, distracting, or annoying.

- Contriving hand movements that look artificial or overly dramatic.

- Choosing gestures that cannot be seen clearly. (A hand motion hidden from audience view by a podium is of no value. Stay in the "honor zone.")

- Leaving their hands in the wrong place for too long.

Keep gestures in the "honor zone" between waist and shoulders.

Your audience should believe that everything you are doing with your face, your hands, your feet, and the space around you is purposeful, yet not forced.

The rules for where you should put your hands have relaxed somewhat. Speech teachers used to have clear lists of "do" and "don't" positions. Now, for example, it may be acceptable to put a hand in your pocket in some speaking environments—but not at the moment when you are making your most serious point. The following are some hand movements you should still avoid:

- Crossing your arms (this may convey defensiveness) or putting your hands on your hips (this can look angry or aggressive).

- Placing your hands in front of you in the "fig leaf" position (especially for male speakers).

- Hooking your fingers together at your ribcage in the "opera singer" pose.

- Gripping the podium (the "white knuckle" syndrome) or clasping your hands behind your back (for more than a moment or two).

USE APPROPRIATE BODY MOVEMENT

Body movement is another important way to bring life to a presentation. Pausing between key points and physically moving to another place in the room helps your listeners know that you have completed one point and are now ready to address another. This is the non-verbal equivalent of a new paragraph. Such pauses and movement help your listeners follow your logical development. If you cannot freely move around, you may still use the pause with a shift in position or a change in the direction you're looking to indicate the same things. Whenever possible, avoid the speaker-behind-the-podium format. If you need a microphone, a cordless, clip-on microphone is best for freedom of movement.

SMILE

Start your presentation with a smile. It relaxes both you and your audience. Look for other appropriate places in your speech when a smile would be appropriate, as well. The rest of the time, use facial expressions to enhance the emotions you are communicating with your message.

A smile is often the best non-verbal expression. It reassures your audience.

We once worked with a very charming corporate executive who was often interviewed by the media. He was always very focused, and his answers were always succinct and articulate. However, when he concentrated, he tended to draw his eyebrows together—his "thinking" face. The resulting expression looked like anger or defensiveness. To develop his skills, he videotaped his performance, and he was shocked at how stern and intense he looked. He learned to dial back the intensity by replacing the "thinking" expression by slightly raising his eyebrows instead of drawing them together. This one change made a dramatic difference in both his interviews and in his interpersonal interactions.

KEEP YOUR WEIGHT ON BOTH FEET

Again, this sounds obvious, but speakers tend to forget that the audience can see their feet. They will cross them, bounce, and rock back and forth, all of which can be terribly distracting. If you concentrate on keeping the weight on the balls of your feet, you will be balanced and ready to move when you want to. Be careful to avoid "dancing"—where you shift the weight from side to side.

USE PHYSICAL SPACE WISELY

The space around you when you speak is yours, so use it to enhance your presentation. The rule about moving around is: walk, or stand still. When you are standing still, stand *completely* still. Do not dance with your feet, your knees, or your shoulders. When you walk, do it for a reason. As we mentioned earlier, changing your position in the room can show a natural break or emphasize a point in the content of your talk. It can also re-attract the audience's attention, allow them to adjust their own physical positions, and give them chance to think about what you are saying.

Use a shift of body position to show a shift in ideas. This can be like a new paragraph in a written message.

SHOW ENTHUSIASM AND CONFIDENCE

Enthusiasm is your most important delivery skill. Audiences and readers will forgive many things, but if you don't seem to care, neither will they.

Assuming you are well-prepared, you should be comfortable expressing enthusiasm about your material. It's okay to let your audience know that you are excited about your topic. And, of course, you focused on your audience's concerns when you selected your specific information, which automatically expresses your enthusiasm for them.

You should also be comfortable expressing enthusiasm about yourself. Show confidence—not cockiness. Believe in yourself—who you are and what you have to offer—what you know and what you are worth. Know that your contributions are right on target because you are experienced and prepared. Then (literally, if you are speaking), you can stand up straight, hold your head up high, and face your audiences head on.

Your audience will forgive many things, but if you don't care, neither will they.

HAVE CONFIDENCE IN YOUR IDEAS

If you have completed your preparation, including thoroughly analyzing your audience and selecting material based on the needs of that audience, you should have confidence in your point of view. The time you invest in the first four steps of the Straight Talk Model always pays off. Avoid the temptation to skip a step. Develop the habit of being thorough and professional in developing your messages. A little extra effort and thought can pay huge dividends in your professionalism.

A little extra preparation and attention to detail can have a dramatic impact on your confidence and communication effectiveness.

REHEARSE AND EDIT

Nothing builds confidence like being well-prepared, even to the point of being over-prepared—totally comfortable with your grasp of the subject matter. And nothing improves the likelihood of speaking success like thorough preparation of the content and delivery of the presentation as well as practice in handling anticipated questions that may arise.

When preparing, put special emphasis on the opening remarks and the conclusion. If you've practiced your opening repeatedly and it goes well, you'll gain confidence for the rest of the presentation. If it doesn't sound so good during your rehearsal, edit it to make it better.

The best way to practice is to work on one section at a time, such as the introduction or the transition from your introduction to your first main point. As we mentioned earlier, don't write your talk word-for-word. If you memorize it, you will sound like you are reciting to the audience rather than having a conversation with them. Instead, practice each section until you are comfortable and fluent. Even if it comes out a little different during the actual presentation, it will still sound natural and spontaneous.

Prepare opening and closing remarks most carefully.

You should also time the presentation to make sure it fits the time allotment or is simply not too long. Audiences are almost always pleasantly surprised when a speech is shorter than expected; they are almost always disappointed when it runs too long.

SELF-CONSCIOUSNESS CAN BECOME SELF-DESTRUCTIVENESS

Over-concern with mechanics once you've reached the point of giving the presentation can only distract and create anxiety. The following is some good advice we have paraphrased from speech experts:

Self-consciousness tends to be self-destructive. If you are overly worried about the way you look, you often overcompensate, and this draws attention to yourself that would not ordinarily be centered on you. It's when you are trying to walk nonchalantly that you walk stiffly or affectedly. It is when you are trying to smile naturally (say "cheese") that your smile tends to look artificial. If you are caught up in conversation or telling a story and the conversation or the story causes you to smile, you are usually unaware of the smile itself, and it is at that point that the smile is, and appears, most natural. So, when you are speaking and get caught up in the message—when you are interested in communicating the ideas to the listeners—you are not usually uncomfortable or noticeably concerned with how you look or how you sound. It's the idea that is at center stage, not the self. Simple remedies: be listener-centered; be message-centered; do not be self-centered.[2]

If possible, videotape your practice. We highly recommend this for important, formal presentations, especially if you are inexperienced. If video is not available, the second best place to work is in front of a large mirror so you can see your non-verbal behavior while you are going over the words. In either case, you can see and hear what works and what you want to improve. Do not practice with *only* an audio-tape recorder. An audio recording without the enhancement of your non-verbal skills is not sufficient feedback.

MANAGE ANXIETY

Relax! Easier said than done, you may say. However, if you are well-prepared and rehearsed, you should be able to relax to a degree where anxiety should not be a problem. You may still feel that brief flush of nervousness just as you are being introduced or beginning your presentation, but it will soon leave because you are prepared. Such nervousness is perfectly natural and is rarely visible to your listeners.

Remember that "stage fright" is normal; it's your body's adrenaline kicking in, which provides extra energy. In fact, speakers who say that they are not nervous at all may face a greater challenge, since an audience might perceive their relaxed attitude as a lack of enthusiasm, or, worse yet, a lack of respect for them.

"Stage fright" is normal and can be useful. It keeps you mentally alert.

OVERCOME ANXIETY SYMPTOMS

Everyone's nerves show in a different place. Here are some tricks for common nervous reactions:

- **Racing heart.** If you have time before your presentation, plan a workout or a run. If your time is limited, find some way to get your heart rate up with some form of exercise like sit-ups, push-ups, squats, or a quick walk to burn off excess energy and take advantage of the extra oxygen.

- **Dry mouth.** Chew your tongue. We know this sounds disgusting, but chewing your tongue creates saliva and helps dry mouth. Don't do it where people can see you—you'll look like a cow.

- **High or weak voice.** Try exercises to improve your voice. Such exercises can make your voice sound stronger or lower-pitched.

EXERCISES FOR VOICE IMPROVEMENT

Try the following simple exercises to build better vocal tone and a stronger-sounding voice:

1 As you are waiting to speak, concentrate on deep breathing. Your lowest natural pitch is supported by good breath-control from your diaphragm. If you are familiar with "yoga breathing," use that (see point 3 below).
2 Concentrate on moving your belt buckle in and out when you inhale and exhale. Don't move your shoulders when you breathe deeply. This heaving motion tightens the muscles around the throat and makes a tight-voice problem worse.
3 Borrow a relaxation strategy from yoga: inhale on four counts, hold for four counts, then exhale for four counts.

- **Shaky hands.** While you are waiting to speak (and while no one is looking), make hard fists and then stretch out your hands several times to increase blood flow and control. However, if you still have the shakes, don't show the audience! Avoid holding up your hands until you get involved with your presentation and calm down.

- **General insecurity.** Stand (or sit) up straight. This is our best all-purpose solution. Nothing conveys personal confidence better than good posture. The extra benefits are that you look more attractive and you can breathe better. Lift your chest, pull your shoulders back and down, and raise your head. Face your audience squarely with your body and look them in the eyes. Smile. You're ready to go.

Keep in mind that, although many of the tips in this chapter seem to refer to presentational speaking (giving speeches or briefings), they also apply in less "formal" communication situations such as interviews or meeting management.

WHEN STAGE FRIGHT FEELS DEBILITATING[3]

Excessive speaking anxiety isn't just found in inexperienced people. One established and otherwise successful business person wrote to one of your authors (Sherron) with this problem:

I am so terrified of giving presentations that I might turn down a better paying job, just because I will be expected to speak in front of groups! I am confident and successful one-on-one and in meetings, but the thought of everyone looking at me standing up there in the spotlight makes me physically sick. How can I get past this fear?

The response from the experienced communication coach went like this:

You are not alone!

The most important thing to remember about presentation anxiety ("stage fright") is this: if you don't have it, you've been dead for several days!

Stage fright is a positive mental and physiological response that creates extra adrenalin. That's a good thing because it fuels your physical energy and your intellectual enthusiasm. Everyone's "speaker nerves" show up differently. For example, even after all my years of presenting, I have insomnia the night before a major event, and I always fret so much about the technology letting me down that I take my presentation on my laptop, on a CD, on a USB drive, and in hard-copy. In your case, the thought of everyone looking at you triggers your presentation anxiety.

First of all, it sounds like you are doing everything right in terms of preparation. If you are confident and successful one-on-one and in meetings, then you obviously are focused and organized with appropriate material to inform or persuade your target audience. Good for you! I usually advise speakers to be certain that they are the primary focus for the audience and that their visual aids are the secondary focus. Visual aids are, after all, "aids"—there to make the presentation clearer for the audience but not to distract.

At the same time, a rule about stage fright is to not let it show. For example, a speaker whose hands shake should not hold them up for the audience to see. Therefore, in your case, to avoid showing your audience that you are nervous, make your visual aids the primary focus of your presentation during the first few minutes until you have your nerves under control.

I would suggest a double attention-grabber—both on the screen and in handouts that you distribute immediately before you begin speaking. If you put something in your audiences' hands, they will look down at it (and not at you). For those who read quickly and look up, have something on the screen that is dramatic, thus once again taking the focus away from you.

Then, as you move through your presentation, be sure that either your slides and handouts are identical or that your handouts supplement the slides with additional detail, so your audience will continue to have something to look at other than you.

> I do not suggest what some speakers choose to do: stand in the dark and use bright slides. Your audience wants to see who is talking rather than just listening to a unidentified voice in the void. But don't worry—they will indeed be looking at your handouts and slides until you are comfortable enough to command their attention.
>
> Appearing nervous is better than appearing dead. Your audience will forgive many things about your delivery skills (while you are working to improve them), but they will never forgive you if you aren't enthusiastic, if you don't appear to care. So learn to use that stage fright to your advantage. Dale Carnegie said it best: "Train your butterflies to fly in formation."
>
> Also remember that, as you improve, it's perfectly okay to use little tricks and to bend the "rules." The end result will be an even more confident and successful speaker: you!

BE YOURSELF AND BECOME YOUR BETTER SELF

Some people who are perfectly comfortable communicating one-on-one believe that they must become someone different when they address a group. They may have seen effective speakers and try to mimic their excellent platform skills. Such emulation can be valuable as you learn delivery techniques from other people, but you should not try to become someone else. Allow your personality to be reflected in all your communication. In brief, be comfortable as yourself. You are as good as anyone, and, because you have prepared your topic, you are likely to be perceived by your audience as the expert on that topic.

> *Your audience will generally perceive you as the expert on your topic.*

Being yourself does not mean that you should disregard the corporate culture of the organization where you are speaking or the social cultures of your audience. You may need to adapt your style. If in doubt, for example, about your casual, energetic style with an unfamiliar audience—particularly an international audience or one made up of individuals considerably older or higher in status than you are—don't try to change your style. Instead, temper your exuberance and try to be a bit more formal in your delivery. As your audience becomes comfortable with you and you build your credibility with your excellent material, you can share your personality with them.

KNOW THAT YOUR AUDIENCE WANTS YOU TO SUCCEED

Your audience doesn't want your presentation to fail. When people have taken the time to hear what you have to say, they don't want to feel their time has been wasted. Even listeners who strongly disagree with you—what we call "hostile listeners"—want you to explain yourself clearly if for no other reason than that they can then attempt to shoot down your ideas.

Your audience wants you to succeed!

A poor presentation can be just as embarrassing and uncomfortable for the audience as it is for the speaker. Think of times that you've seen people do a poor job of expressing an idea. What has your reaction been? You probably felt some embarrassment for those persons and may have found yourself trying to rephrase their ideas for them. Remember that no one is out to get you. Just as you want speakers to succeed, your listeners want you to succeed.

KNOW THAT YOU AND YOUR AUDIENCE NEED EACH OTHER

Every presentation begins with the listener needing something. By coming to your presentation (or interview, briefing) or inviting you to talk, listeners are expressing a need for information, friendship, help, approval, clarification—maybe even inspiration. They hope that something you say will improve their lives.

You as a presenter have needs, too. Probably the strongest need is for approval. Only your listeners can give you this. They can give you such approval in many forms, from a simple vote (a raising of hands) to a signature on a document (a sales agreement) to an outburst of applause or a hearty thank you. Without some indication of approval, response, endorsement, confirmation—*something!*—you'll feel lost at sea, adrift, seeking a signal. This can be tough on the ego. (*No response is in many ways worse than outright rejection.*)

> *No response from our listeners is the most uncomfortable outcome we can experience.*

Since listeners need what you have to offer—information, suggestions, instructions, a welcome, or entertainment—and you need what they offer— approval, appreciation, or applause—work together to create a circle of rapport. A good presenter is like a swan—calm and serene on the surface and paddling like crazy underneath. Remember these pointers, and you can look and sound confident about your message content, your organization, yourself, and about handling unforeseen objections or other surprises.

REMEMBER FEEDBACK AND CONSTANT IMPROVEMENT

Getting feedback is a critical part of the Straight Talk Model and is the key to becoming your better self. Keep in mind that improvement of delivery skills is a life-long project, and the guidelines we have discussed in this chapter are just ways to get you moving in the right direction. [...]

Continue to polish your verbal and non-verbal skills and to develop a style that meets your audience's expectations consistent with the corporate culture. Speak clearly and expressively. Dress professionally. Exhibit control with appropriate facial expressions, hand gestures, and body movement. Prove that you know your material by thoroughly rehearsing in advance. Be comfortable with your notes and your visual aids. Be prepared to answer questions. Express confidence in your material, based on your preparation. Display confidence in yourself through your professionalism and enthusiasm. Most importantly, be yourself. You are who the audience came to see. You are the most important part of your message, and your unique personality is your most valuable platform skill.

As Brenda in our opening story discovered, oral communication skills are very much at the core of many jobs. She was doing fine in her interview for the job but suddenly found herself outside her comfort zone when realizing that she'd be required to present professionally to her new vice-president. This need not be the case.

Once you gain control over your anxiety, you, like Brenda, have the opportunity to dazzle your audience with good verbal and non-verbal skills, platform management, and a projection of confidence that is the hallmark of professionalism. By applying each step of the Straight Talk Model, you can achieve considerable success in delivering oral messages with confidence and impact.

PERFORMANCE CHECKLIST

After completing this chapter, you should be better able to apply some principles for selecting and organizing information for your message. Specifically, you should now understand that:

- Delivering effective oral messages depends on your ability to polish your verbal and non-verbal delivery skills, develop your platform-management skills, show confidence and enthusiasm, rehearse and edit, manage anxiety and express confidence to be yourself and become your better self.

- Polishing your verbal delivery skills includes speaking clearly and expressively, paying attention to timing, avoiding distracting vocal patterns, and minimizing verbalized pauses.

- Polishing your platform-management skills includes using notes and visuals effectively and handling audience questions constructively.

- Words that you emphasize can change the meaning of your sentences; listen carefully to avoid unintended hidden meanings.

- Polishing your non-verbal delivery skills includes maintaining eye contact, displaying a professional image, and exhibiting physical control.

- Expressing confidence and enthusiasm is accomplished by practicing your material, being idea-conscious, and knowing that you and your audience meet needs for each other.

- Being yourself and becoming your better self are functions of a sensitivity to the speaking context (especially the culture) and of feedback you can apply to improve.

WHAT DO YOU KNOW?

ACTIVITY 7.1: TAKING A SELF-INVENTORY

Oral communication skills and attitudes improve through evaluation—by others and by you. This self-inventory identifies your starting point. It will be useful to you only to the degree to which you are totally honest in your answers. You need not show this to others. Use it as an honest look within yourself. You may want to re-take it after you have applied the skills discussed in this book to develop your communication skills further.

The following checklist shows how you see yourself as an oral communicator. Read each statement and circle "yes" or "no." After answering "yes" or "no," review each answer and circle the (+) or (–) to indicate how you feel about your answer. A plus means you are satisfied; a minus means you wish you could have answered otherwise.

Answer honestly based upon how you actually feel or act, not how you wish you would.

1. Before I enter into an important communication event, I often think carefully about the context, audiences, culture, and my objectives.
   yes no (+) (–)

2. I often have great ideas I'd like to share with other people.
   yes no (+) (–)

3. I enjoy trying to explain my ideas to others.
   yes no (+) (–)

4. I often get the conversation going among my friends and even with people I don't know.
   yes no (+) (–)

5. When I stand up to speak in any group, I feel excited (but not overly anxious).
   yes no (+) (–)

6. Before trying to influence others, I make it a point to be certain that I know as much as possible about my audience(s).
   yes no (+) (–)

7. I am good at persuading others to my views.

yes no (+) (−)

8. I am comfortable and efficient in preparing visual aids (PowerPoint™ slides, etc.).

   yes no (+) (−)

9. I communicate my feelings and ideas well and therefore have influence in my job and social settings.

   yes no (+) (−)

10. I like to teach groups of people new things.

    yes no (+) (−)

11. I enjoy planning ways to simplify and present ideas so others will understand them.

    yes no (+) (−)

12. When communicating, I consider audience feelings and attitudes to be at least as important as facts and ideas.

    yes no (+) (−)

13. In comparison with my colleagues or associates, I think I speak more clearly and carefully than they do.

    yes no (+) (−)

14. I have a good vocabulary and can phrase ideas well.

    yes no (+) (−)

15. My physical delivery (use of hands, posture, expressiveness) is one of my strongest communication skills.

    yes no (+) (−)

16. My voice has good variation, is pleasant, and conveys enthusiasm well.

    yes no (+) (−)

17. I am eager to hear helpful criticism from others after I speak.

    yes no (+) (−)

18. Improving my oral communication skills is one of my highest priorities.

    yes no (+) (−)

19. I have the basic qualities needed to be an excellent oral communicator.

    yes no (+) (−)

20. I speak clearly and pronounce words correctly.

    yes no (+) (−)

21 People seem to enjoy what I say; I hold their interest.
    yes no (+) (−)

22 I use humor and story-telling effectively.
    yes no (+) (−)

23 I handle audience questions very well.
    yes no (+) (−)

24 I feel that I am getting better and better in my communication skills.
    yes no (+) (−)

25 After a communication experience, I review what I should have done differently to create a positive outcome.
    yes no (+) (−)

Now, review your self-inventory. For each item where you circled a minus sign (indicating that you don't feel good about your answer), write a goal for personal improvement. Your goal should be specific and clear. For example, if you write a goal for statement 4, you might say, "I will start conversations with one person I don't know each day this week." For statement 16, you might say, "I will work for greater vocal variation to hold listener interest." For statement 22, you might say, "I will practice incorporating more stories in my presentations and conversations."

Write your goals in the spaces below. If you have more than five areas to work on, put them in order of importance. Then write your top five goals here:

Goal 1: _____
Goal 2: _____
Goal 3: _____
Goal 4: _____
Goal 5: _____

For each goal you have set above, sketch out an action plan and timeline for its accomplishment. Be specific about the activities needed to achieve the goal. Where will you get the knowledge you need? How will you gain the experiences needed for growth? Be specific about what you will do.

ACTIVITY 7.2: EVALUATING A SUCCESSFUL SPEAKER

Attend a live speech or view one on TV or video. (The speaker may be someone you know personally, a business or political leader, a member of the clergy, a television show host, or anyone who makes a living doing oral presentations.) Take notes during the presentation. Look for applications (or misapplications) of the ideas in this chapter. Then write a brief description of the speaker, commenting on this person's delivery style. Suggest ways he or she could improve.

ACTIVITY 7.3: PREPARING A TEAM PRESENTATION

1. As a team, select a company that is internationally known and that is currently managing multiple challenges. (Some examples: the airline industry, pharmaceutical regulation issues, corporate ethics scandals, product recalls, employee discrimination suits, etc.)
2. Assume that you are a communication consulting team and your job is to advise the company or organization on how best to handle the communication aspects of their challenges.
3. Working in a team, develop a presentation to persuade your target audience to take a specific course of action.
4. Prepare computer-projected visual aids for your presentation.
5. Practice your presentation based on the information in this chapter.
6. Before you present, be prepared to tell the class about your target audience so they can role-play and ask you questions as if they were that audience.
7. Keep the presentation to ten minutes plus a question-and-answer session. Remember to close with your final statement; don't let the Q&A be the final thing your audience hears.

ACTIVITY 7.4: PREPARING A "HOW-TO" PRESENTATION

Prepare a four-to-six-minute "how-to" presentation. To get double benefit from this presentation, select a topic that teaches how to improve speaking effectiveness. Some examples are:

PRESENTATION EVALUATION

SPEAKER:
TOPIC:
SPEAKER'S TARGET AUDIENCE:
EVALUATOR:

Directions for the speaker: evaluate yourself on each point before you present.
Directions for evaluator: evaluate the speaker on each point.

	Good	Needs Work
CONTENT		
Uses relevant material for audience's knowledge level		
Acknowledges audience's wants and concerns		
Has sufficient depth in support material		
Uses interesting examples for audience and situation		
Uses appropriate visual aids (if appropriate)		
ORGANIZATION		
Grabs audience's attention		
States clear agenda		
Includes benefit in introduction		
Follows clear organizational plan		
Summarizes essence of main points		
Asks for clear action in conclusion		
Closes with strong final statement		
DELIVERY		
Moves comfortably and gestures naturally		
Looks at each member of the audience		
Speaks conversationally and enthusiastically (vocal variation)		
Handles visual aids effectively		

Overall comments:
Finally, what is the likelihood that you would buy this product, hire this person, or support this proposal? Why, or why not?

Figure 7.1 Presentation Evaluation Worksheet

- How to use gestures for greater communication effectiveness.

- How to use vocal variation.

- How to reduce speaker anxiety.

- How to dress for a business presentation for your organization.

- How to create and use humor in a presentation.

- How to create an effective introduction (or conclusion).

- How to handle questions and answers after a presentation.

You are not limited to the topics listed above, but your presentation must be communication-related. Apply the ideas discussed in this chapter. Practice in front of a mirror.

ACTIVITY 7.5: SELLING A PRODUCT

Develop and deliver an effective five-minute sales pitch. Select a product or service that would be appropriate to sell to a person who is just completing graduate school and is beginning a new business career. This should be a real product (or service) and should sell for not more than $300.

Apply a persuasive pattern of arrangement [...] and be prepared to explain why you structured the presentation as you did. If possible, videotape your delivery and review it with a colleague or your boss. Ask for concrete feedback. (Invite your evaluator to use the form in Figure 7.1. Also fill out a self-critique based on your viewing of your tape.)

REINFORCE WITH THESE REVIEW QUESTIONS

1. True/False—Verbalized pauses or "filler words" are helpful in that they keep the flow of information constant.
2. True/False—"Up-speak" makes statements sound like questions, thus undermining the perception of speaker confidence.
3. In addition to verbal skills, communicators should be aware of their _____ and _____ skills as well.
4. True/False—Speaking expressively involves putting the emphasis on the right words in a sentence.
5. When using visual aids in a presentation, maintain your focus on your _____.
6. The three steps to answering questions (and avoiding rambling) are:
   (1) _____,
   (2) _____, and
   (3) _____.
7. True/False—When speaking to a group, scanning over the whole audience is a good way to build eye contact.
8. Nothing reduces anxiety like being well _____.
9. True/False—Being idea-conscious can help overcome being self-conscious.
10. True/False—You are the most important part of your message and your unique personality is your most valuable platform skill.

MINI-CASE STUDY

When Andrew walked into the conference room, all he could think was, "I feel like a donkey in the Kentucky Derby. I shouldn't be here talking to these big-shot, successful people. I'm going to look and sound like a total idiot."

Andrew is the Facilities Manager for Ajax Credit Union. His job is to be certain that the buildings and facilities for the company's 12 branch offices are kept in tip-top condition. It's a complex and demanding job for which Andrew earned a degree from the local State College. But somehow, Andrew, despite his considerable expertise in all aspects of building planning and maintenance, still feels like, as he puts it, "a glorified janitor."

Now the Board of Directors has asked him to come to their monthly meeting and talk about the remodeling of several branches. He knows what to tell them and feels that he will be able to answer any questions, but he is still, well, freaked out by the thought of standing up and delivering his message.

QUESTIONS

1. If Andrew came to you and expressed these fears, what would you tell him?
2. Describe three specific ways Andrew could best prepare for his presentation.
3. What, if anything, would you advise Andrew to avoid?

NOTES

1 Michael Waldhold, "Here's One Reason, Uh, Smart People Say 'Uh'," *Wall Street Journal*, March 19, 1991, p. B1.

2 This time-tested approach was discussed in the classic speech text by Harold P. Zelco and Frank E. X. Dance, *Business and Professional Speech Communication*, 2nd ed. (Austin: Holt, Rhinehart and Winston, 1978), pp. 77–79.

3 Originally published in Dr. Sherron Bienvenu's online Communication Solutions newsletter, September 2004.

CHAPTER SUMMARY

As we can see in the reading, preparation is one of the key components in our ability to maintain strong confidence in our delivery of a speech. We need to make sure that we carefully walk through all of the different steps in the public speaking process prior to delivery to give ourselves, and our audience, the reassurance that we know what we are talking about. With this in mind, we are able to exhibit enthusiasm and confidence in our delivery and provide our audience a reason why they should listen to us. Confidence and enthusiasm are two important pieces in channeling our nervousness and anxiety into positive energy that's useful in successfully getting our message across and keeping our audience engaged. The next time you are about to speak before an audience, remind yourself of the excitement you have about delivering a speech to the audience and your confidence in your ability to present the information.

CHAPTER 8

ARE YOU READY TO SPEAK PUBLICLY?

Throughout this text, we have discussed the intricacies of nervousness and anxiety and what that looks like for different individuals. We considered the possibilities of leveraging our anxiety as positive energy to be used in delivering speeches. We also examined the biology and psychology of nervousness as well as the relationship between anxiety and public speaking. We took a look at utilizing meditation as a useful tool in maintaining control and using mindfulness to center ourselves, in addition to employing confidence in our abilities as public speakers. With all of this in mind, the question then becomes: Are you ready to speak publicly?

In this chapter, we provide final thoughts and guidelines for you to employ on the day of your presentation or speech, and we summarize and reinforce many of the concepts discussed earlier in the text in regard to managing your nervousness when speaking in public. In the reading, "Pause and Refresh—Relax, You'll Do Fine," you are provided with a useful outline of what a typical day looks like when one has to deliver a speech. This reading also provides many additional recommendations to consider, not only prior to the delivery of the speech but also during the presentation itself.

PAUSE AND REFRESH— RELAX, YOU'LL DO FINE

by Association for Talent Development

OVERVIEW

Using techniques to steady your nerves
Harnessing the power of positive thinking
Preparing on the day of the presentation
Handling emergencies while presenting
Managing Q&A sessions

Does the thought of having to give a presentation immediately bring up thoughts of stage fright, presentation jitters, nervousness, butterflies, fretting, anxiety, and foreboding? If so, keep in mind that it is natural to be nervous before giving a presentation. Almost everyone gets butterflies—the trick is to harness this nervous energy and direct it into delivering a stellar presentation.

Whatever you do, do not start off by saying, "Whew, am I nervous!" and broadcasting your fear. Participants will then look for nervous signals during your presentation rather than listening to your message. The tips and tricks offered in this chapter can help you to steady your nerves and get in the right frame of mind prior to stepping on the podium.

"Pause and Refresh—Relax, You'll Do Fine," *10 Steps to Successful Presentation Skills*, pp. 153-168. Copyright © 2008 by Association for Talent Development (ATD). Reprinted with permission.

USING TECHNIQUES TO STEADY YOUR NERVES AND MAKE YOUR PRESENTATION A SUCCESS

An expectant hush falls on the crowd. Offstage, the speaker breathes deeply. The introducer's voice rings clearly through the giant room, giving brief highlights of the speaker's credentials. The speaker strides confidently to the stage, pauses, looks out across the audience, and begins.

The presentation is an ideal blend of intriguing topic and informative content, which inspires a sense of immediacy in the listeners. A preview of the key points helps the audience listen most effectively. Each key point is supported by distilled information and vivid examples. The content brims with value, relevance, and timeliness; the delivery is animated, yet relaxed. The presenter uses a compelling voice, direct eye contact, and occasional humor to engage and hold the audience. Visuals, handouts, and reference material reinforce the message. Audience questions are handled with skill, intelligence, and respect. The presentation finishes with a challenge and a call to action.

One technique—as illustrated in the example above—called "visualization," is used by many successful presenters to rehearse in their heads not only the flow of the presentation but also how the presenter delivers the content as well as the audience's reaction at each point in the speech.

Remember, it's normal to be nervous. In fact, if you aren't at least a little nervous, you need to seriously question whether you are ready to give a presentation, because nerves give you the "edge" that often gets the adrenaline going and can make the difference between a good presentation and an outstanding, engaging presentation!

Use these additional techniques to help steady your nerves before the presentation:

- **Plan what you are going to wear**—plan to wear something that you always feel comfortable in, that should be a little more formal than the most formally dressed person you expect in the audience. Do not choose to wear anything new the day of the presentation, including suits, haircuts, shoes, jewelry, and so on. If you are uncomfortable, it will add to your nervousness and distract you from the task at hand.

- **Try to arrive at least 15–30 minutes early**—to familiarize yourself with your surroundings and the layout of the room, to ensure that the room is set up as planned, and to deal with any potential issues (for example, are the audiovisual aids available and working).

- **Use a preparation checklist**—have a "cheat sheet checklist" ready to go so that you have a standard routine that includes checking all audiovisual equipment, room setup, other logistics, additional information from the sponsor (e.g., we need to shave 10 minutes off your presentation or we need you to speak 20 minutes longer than planned), revised numbers of participants, handling of late arrivals, getting a glass or bottle of water, and anything else that will alleviate possible pot holes.

- **Use a crutch to help you with the flow or key points**—for some presenters, crutches might be audiovisual aids, flipcharts, or notes formatted with specific colors, highlighted text, and so on. Whatever works for you, don't be afraid to use crutches to help keep you grounded on the flow of the topics and key points. If you get distracted or lose your place in the presentation your crutch will help to get you back on track.

- **Do some deep breathing**—use deep-breathing techniques by inhaling through your nose, holding your breath for a few seconds, and slowly exhaling through your mouth. This technique gets more oxygen circulating throughout your body and your brain.

- **Do some warm-up exercises**—along with deep breathing while out of sight of the audience (for example, waiting to be introduced), do some head or shoulder rolls, arm- and side-stretches, or even a few toe touches to stretch, warm up your body, and relax. For example, pull your shoulders up toward your ears and then push them down. Shake out cold hands to stimulate them and warm them up. If you can't do any of these because you are in front of the audience, take one last deep breath before speaking into the mike.

- **Envision the first 90 seconds**—use your visualization technique to play the first 90 seconds of your presentation in your head again to get you focused.

- **Greet audience members as they arrive**—depending on the size of the audience, this may or may not be feasible. If you can meet and greet the participants as they enter, this may help to reduce your stress level and provide you with insight into their motivation for attending.

- **You lose your place or an audience member asks a "stumper" question**—it is OK to take a few seconds to find your place, gather your thoughts or ponder a question that someone has asked. Consider calmly taking a sip of water, glancing at your notes, or formulating your answer to a sticky question. Sometimes "pregnant pauses" not only allow you to gather your thoughts but also allow the audience members to noodle over the question asked or the information presented. Keep in mind that presenters usually speak faster than audience members can process the information, so slight pauses not only help you, but also allow the audience time to think as well.

HARNESSING THE POWER OF POSITIVE THINKING

Positive thinking helps with stress management and can even improve your presentation delivery. Positive thinking focuses on being optimistic in your approach and attitude.

So how can you put this into action to develop successful presentation skills? Positive thinking focuses on "self-talk," which is the stream of thoughts running through your mind every day. These thoughts can be positive or negative. So when you are going to present—don't waste energy imagining everything that could go wrong. Rather, focus on how this presentation is going to "wow" the audience!

For example, if you are worried about giving your presentation and are visualizing that you will trip across the stage, your notes will fall and be out of order, you will lose your place in the presentation, or crumble when an audience member asks a challenging question—what do you think is most likely going to happen when you take the stage?

It's important to differentiate between negative and positive self-talk. Compare "I'll never be able to get up before that group and explain to them the new benefits package" with "I know what I'm talking about, and I can give this presentation so that the others will understand this new benefits package too." Using positive self-talk (and being prepared, of course) increases your chances of accomplishing your goal by quantum leaps.

Positive thinking requires behavior change and creating new habits—so just like any change, this takes time and practice. Periodically during the day, stop and reflect on what you are thinking about. Are your thoughts positive or negative? If you find that they are mostly negative, then stop and find a way to put a positive spin on them.

Focus on the visualization technique mentioned earlier in this chapter. In your mind's eye, do a "run through" of the presentation. Visualize how you want it to flow, what you plan to say, when you plan to use the visual aids, and so on. By focusing on the best delivery scenario, you will be on your way to implementing positive thinking and visualizing success!

> **POINTER**
> Positive thinking focuses on being positive in your approach and attitude. Don't waste energy imagining everything that could go wrong.

PREPARING ON THE DAY OF THE PRESENTATION

On presentation day, plan to wear something:

- comfortable

- compatible with the color(s) of whatever will be behind you

- solid in color or with a small, overall pattern

- bright (for example, such as a bright-red tie or scarf near your face)

- similar to the most formal outfit you would expect audience members to wear.

Avoid

- excessive food or caffeinated beverages

- alcohol

- over-the-counter medications that may make you drowsy or hyperactive.

Remember to bring

- your note cards or pages in duplicate

- several handkerchiefs

- a small tape recorder and tape (if the sponsor hasn't arranged for professional audio- or videotaping)

- an emergency telephone number to call if you're delayed or need directions after you're on the way to the presentation location.

Keep in mind the following:

- You are always speaking to individuals no matter how many people are in the audience.

POINTER

Ten+ Deadly Mistakes

Research conducted by Meeting Planners International indicates that there are 12 presenting "sins" that prompt attendees to walk out, criticize programs harshly, send letters of complaint, or ask for their money back. They are

- Appearing unprepared
- Handling questions inappropriately
- Apologizing for self or organization
- Being unaware of current public information in his or her field
- Using unprofessional audiovisual aids
- Seeming to be off-schedule—especially failing to end on time
- Not involving attendees
- Not establishing personal rapport
- Appearing disorganized
- Not starting off quickly with impact
- Selling from the professional platform
- Using sexist or racist comments, ethnic slurs, or inappropriate humor.

- To some degree, audience members have different backgrounds, and some of them may have different private problems you can't see (such as a toothache). Nobody (to paraphrase Lincoln) "can please all of the people, all of the time," so if a few people in the audience look grumpy or pained, it probably has nothing to do with the quality of your presentation.

- Chances are, people who've made the effort to come to the presentation want to hear what you have to say and want you to succeed.

- You've done your homework—so you know what you're talking about.

- Nervous energy is a natural high that energizes speakers who don't worry about it. If your excitement threatens to turn to jitters, use up excess energy with a few small exercises or breathing techniques.

HANDLING EMERGENCIES WHILE PRESENTING

Here are some quick tips and tricks of what to do if

- **You perspire profusely**—wipe your face with a handkerchief. Do it firmly, do not dab. Avoid using a tissue since it may shred and stick to your face.

- **Your hands shake**—rest them on the lectern but don't put a death grip on it!

- **Your knees wobble**—do nothing. If you're behind a lectern, no one can see. If you're at the head of a runway, walk around a bit; the shaking will stop.

- **You need to cough, sneeze, or clear your throat**—turn away from the mike; go ahead and cough. If necessary, take a sip of water before you begin again. Say "As I was saying . . ."

- **Your nose starts to run**—Say "Excuse me," turn from the mike, and blow your nose. Don't be dainty or you'll just have to do it again soon. Turn back to the mike and continue your speech. Bring two or three handkerchiefs with you, just in case.

- **You notice the audience's chairs aren't facing the lectern**—if the chairs aren't bolted down, start by saying, "I think you'll be more comfortable if your chairs are facing the speaker's stand. So, before I get started, why don't you turn them around?" Wait until the hubbub dies down, then start as you planned.

- **The audience knowledge varies and they know more than you**—knowing how much knowledge or expertise your audience has regarding the subject of your presentation will affect the breadth and depth of your presentation. At times, you might not have a good feel for this until you are meeting and greeting some of the audience members. You will need to determine if the audience needs to hear everything you are prepared to present or if you should employ the KISS principle ("keep it simple, stupid!). If the audience expertise varies widely, try to approach the topic from a middle-ground perspective so that you provide new information to novices and sprinkle in more advanced information to provide something new to those who already have baseline knowledge of the topic. You can always adjust the pace and depth of the presentation downward, to ensure you are reaching as many people as possible. If several audience members possess PhDs and they have garnered accolades from peers or the industry on the topic, don't panic. When appropriate, solicit opinions and try to draw some of these "experts" into the discussion. Don't give control over to them—but by recognizing their expertise and opinions, you can build potential allies on the subject.

- **You are presenting to organizational superiors**—if the audience includes your superiors or C-level executives, involve these participants by asking them to share personal experiences about the topic, for example, which leadership traits they find most useful in their roles as managers. By establishing and encouraging this dynamic, you assume a facilitator role that builds credibility, shows off your skills, and takes the pressure off you for being the sole source of content and ideas.

MANAGING Q&A SESSIONS

Questions asked during the presentation have two purposes:

- to clarify matters that are for any reason unclear to the audience

- to engage an audience, secure their presentation, and maintain communication.

No matter what the purpose is for the question-and-answer session, you will need to stay in command of the session the entire time. Use these best practices to maintain control and effectively manage the Q&A session.

- Anticipate questions the audience is likely to ask. Plan short, to-the-point answers.

- Announce that you'll be taking questions for 20 minutes (or whatever time is

> **POINTER**
> No matter what the purpose for the Q&A session is, you need to stay in command the entire time.

  allotted), then say you'll wait a few minutes for those who need to leave now to pack up and go.

- Invite questions by saying something like, "Let's get started. Now, what questions do you have? To give as many people as possible a chance to speak, please limit your question to one minute."

- Arrange for someone you know to ask the lead-off question. Hearing someone else from the audience speak first gives other audience members time to think and psychological permission to take the floor. Admit that you know the questioner. Say, "I see my friend Sue's hand out there. Yes, Sue?"

- Call on people in different areas of the audience. If audience members might be categorized by gender, age, or ethic group, don't exclude that group. Also give each person you call on "equal time" up to the established limit.

- Listen with a neutral expression. Make eye contact with the question-asker, but avoid smiling, frowning, or nodding "yes" or "no." If you say, "That's a good question" to some people, those who do not win this praise may be disappointed. If you praise every question, you'll sound insincere.

- Stop long-winded question-askers. Break eye contact. Hold up your hand to indicate "stop." Say, "Let me respond to that." Say it twice if necessary. If a questioner still continues, handle this person like a heckler.

- Repeat questions through your mike unless:

  - Question-askers have mikes of their own.

  - Part of the question is something you don't want to be quoted as saying. If you repeat, "Why does XYZ Corp. fire older workers instead of retraining them?" expect to hear on the news that you said "XYZ Corp. fires older workers instead of retraining them."

- Be prepared to say, "I can't answer that question because it assumes (whatever) while I believe (whatever to the contrary). This will save you from the issue mentioned above. Instead, say, "I can't answer that because you assume workers' ages were a factor. Actually, the recent layoffs were based on.... And workers were selected for retraining based on..."

- Divide multipart questions. Answer the parts separately.

- Don't challenge question-askers with "Why do you ask?" If a question seems vague or rambling, say "Could you restate that?" If after the restatement you still don't get the point, use a phrase from the restatement to construct a question that you are prepared to answer.

- Relate answers to the main point of the speech when possible.

- Control the last words the audience hears. Say, "We just have time for one or two more questions." If your next answer goes particularly well, end the session. If the question and answer are off the main point of the presentation, finish by restating the key point of the presentation.

Generating questions usually falls in a question-and-answer session at the end of the presentation. The traditional Q&A starts with the presenter asking, "Are there any questions?" However, this method may intimidate and inhibit audience members who have very serious questions from asking them in a large-group setting.

To facilitate listeners to ask questions, presenters often ask the audience to "anonymously" write questions on 3-by-5-inch cards that are passed to the speaker.

In other presentation formats, question-askers may line up at a microphone positioned at the head of the aisle before your presentation. This microphone is usually *not* activated until after your presentation. If that is the case, keep in mind that you may need to switch the "audience" microphone on from the lectern or turn it off if a participant becomes verbally abusive or refuses others to access the mike.

In other situations, someone with a hand mike may hold it out to audience members you have recognized for questions, or you may have the only microphone in the room.

When responding to participant questions:

- Honor each question with a direct answer. Support answers with specifics.

- Divide any complicated questions into understandable parts and deal with each part.

- When listeners ask a question in front of the group, recognize them and reiterate the question to confirm that you understand what they are asking and to ensure that everyone in the audience heard the question being asked.

- Quickly defer irrelevant questions, but do it pleasantly.

- Recognize questioners from all parts of the room, not just those who might be in the front.

Knowing that you are prepared and have considered everything you need for your presentation will enable you to focus and be calm. Use Tool 8.1 to verify that you have taken care of everything so you can be at ease.

TOOL 8.1
Countdown-to-Successful-Presentations Checklist

Use this final countdown checklist to help you relax and ensure that everything will go off without a hitch on presentation day!

2+ Weeks Before the Presentation (Start as soon as possible!)
- ☐ Tackle the list of 5W questions to determine the purpose of the presentation and conduct an informal audience analysis.
- ☐ Make the room arrangements including equipment, supplies, refreshments, etc.
- ☐ Create your presentation and visual aids.

- Select the type of facilitation techniques you want to use to create session interactivity.
- Develop the specific questions to ask the audience and anticipate audience questions and your planned response.
- Make a list of all supporting presentation materials that you need.
- Put together and confirm that you have everything needed in your presenter's resource / risk management kit [...].
- Do a run through and fine-tune your presentation and notes.

One Week Before the Presentation
- Confirm that you have the right date and time of the presentation.
- Confirm that the room and set-up arrangements will be ready for presentation day.
- Rehearse your presentation with a friendly critic and ask for feedback and ideas.
- Make any final adjustments to your notes and confirm that you have a backup set of notes ready to go.
- Memorize the first 90 seconds of your presentation and how you plan to introduce each key point during the presentation.
- Practice using all audiovisuals including practicing with your flipcharts, switching to overhead transparencies, or presentation software slides. Be sure to click through all of the slides to remember where any special effects—such as dissolves, animation, or sounds—occur in relation to your notes. Check for any misspellings.
- Pick out the clothes you plan to wear—remember, wear what you are going to be most comfortable in (preferably nothing new) that is slightly more formal than your audience.
- Send presentation materials and any supplies ahead of time and call to be sure that they arrived.
- Confirm the directions for the meeting location.
- Exchange phone numbers with the sponsor or contact person for the event—especially if you are flying in.
- Double-check your presenter's toolkit [...] and replenish the supplies as needed.
- Use your visualization techniques and positive self-talk to run through your presentation in your mind's eye and visualize success.

Presentation Day
- Arrive at least 30 minutes to 1 hour prior to your presentation time.
- Verify the presentation room location.

- ☐ Identify the on-site audiovisual contact or how to contact the presentation sponsor.
- ☐ Ask to have the box of materials that you sent ahead delivered if it is not already in the presentation room.
- ☐ Test all equipment.
- ☐ Tape down cords or power strips to prevent tripping hazards.
- ☐ Focus all equipment.
- ☐ Test the microphones, if necessary.
- ☐ Set the volume controls for microphones and any audiovisual aids.
- ☐ Have the extra set of note cards ready in your pocket and a set in place on the lectern.
- ☐ Organize your space for handouts and your presentation supplies such as markers, tape, and so on.
- ☐ Get a glass or bottle of water and paper towels.
- ☐ Scout out the restroom location.
- ☐ Arrange participant handouts either at their seats or at the end of the aisles for quick distribution either at the beginning or end of the presentation.
- ☐ Tidy up the room by hiding empty boxes, etc.

Before you Present
- ☐ Review the first 90 seconds of your opening.
- ☐ Do your deep breathing and stretching techniques to help you relax.
- ☐ Run through your visualization and envision success and how you want the session to flow.
- ☐ Greet the participants.
- ☐ Present a memorable conclusion.

NOTES

NOTES

CHAPTER SUMMARY

Public speaking can be a very stressful and challenging task that many of us will have to endure at multiple times in our personal and professional lives. Understanding our own anxieties, and examining how they impact our ability to complete this task, is one of the first steps in truly managing our nervousness when speaking publicly. Now, armed with this wealth of knowledge and this new sense of confidence in yourself and your abilities to speak publicly, get out there and let your voice be heard!

Printed by Libri Plureos GmbH in Hamburg, Germany